This work is subject to copyrights. Nothing in this work maybe reproduced in any form, in parts or as a whole, without express written permission from the author.

© 2013 Martijn Sjoorda

Table of Contents

Introduction	6
Acknowledgements	15
Problems	18
Fragmentation	19
Stacking	20
Sometimes you need to slow down	21
Cracking The Code	23
Organisations, why bother?	24
Big Idea	27
Impeding Convictions	28
Implications for organising work	29
Roles for organisations	30
Taking Stock	41
Dialogue	46
Craft # 1 – Dialogue	53
Framing Systemic Challenges	56
Design	58
Craft # 2 – Systems Thinking	61
Conditions For Success	64
Strategy is underrated	65
Making strategy is a process	66
Interdependency	66
Two really large chunks	72

Face the brutal facts	77
Enough is enough	78
Sit on your hands and bite your tongue	79

Teams   80

Level 1 – Action Domain	84
Level 2 – Language	85
Level 3 – Operating System	87
Level 4 – Heroic Mode	88
Craft #3 – Understanding Team Dynamics	91

Personal   94

Craft #4 – Personal (Story) Work	101

Making It Work   108

Rule #6	109
Purpose, Strategy & Key Behaviours	112
Create Leaders of Leaders	114
Build Your Rhythm	118
Play To Win	119
Exceed & Excel	121

About the author   124

Recommended further reading   126

Consulted literature   128

Notes   130

Tech – no – lo –gy:

==The use of tools, machines, materials, techniques, and sources of power to make work easier and more productive.==

The Cambridge Encyclopedia, David Crystal (Ed.), Cambridge University Press (1990).

This book contains a distillation of some five areas of what I dubbed *human process technology*. In addition to the definition of technology above, someone once argued that technology only has the right to be called that if it is subject to continuous improvement, is reproducible and produces predictable results.

If you learn, through becoming a craftsman (f/m) at these practices, you can deliver this.

Introduction

"Ring the bells – ring the bells that still can ring. Forget your perfect offering. There is a crack – a crack in everything. That's how the light gets in."

- "Anthem" – Leonard Cohen

We spend more time in organizations than we do with our loved ones and friends. Yet we treat them as a parallel universe where the rules of being human only apply loosely. This is detrimental to people and organizations. Because we do this, we short-change the companies we work for and ourselves as well. Many people feel compelled to adopt a mask that leaves 70% of who they are out at the workplace. In doing so we collectively settle for mediocrity instead of a high-performance meritocracy. We do so because organizations often create a context that causes us to tap into fear, lack of trust and other negative dynamics rather than incite us to follow our natural drive to stand for something, look for what is healthy and drive for results on the basis of applied common sense.

In my work as an advisor to companies I meet so many people who are disillusioned about their workplace. If I ask them why, the answer invariably starts with "They…" or "It…" Paradoxically, people that are on the work floor are often as disillusioned as their senior leaders. While they are part of the same organization and they all show up with the best intentions, they often fail to break through this standoff. They fail to crack the code. This is what I get out of bed for and it's the topic and purpose of this book: to provide simple human process technology that can help leaders crack the code. So we can make organizations much nicer, healthier places to be in. Because I believe that doing so will set them up to achieve great things. Life is not meant to be lived in a mediocre way and mediocre organizations don't have a great track record of survival.

It's frequently hard, but in the last 12 years we have proven many times over with our clients that it is possible. It does require us to "unlearn" some of the things we take for granted or accept as best practices in organisations.

This book offers a few lenses and tools to help you crack the code. By way of introduction I will share some of my personal history. Firstly, because that constitutes eating my own medicine: I contend that showing up as who you are, just that, warts and all, is precisely enough. Gaining a deeper understanding of your personal story, how the patterns that have emerged from that influence you in how you lead and sharing these with colleagues will make you a lot more successful and effective as a leader.

Conventional wisdom holds that getting close to employees can compromise objectivity and the ability to make tough management decisions. "I dramatically disagree with that," Sandberg says. "I believe in bringing your whole self to work. We are who we are. When you try to have this division between your personal self and professional self, what you really are is stiff... That doesn't mean people have to tell me everything about their personal lives. But I'm pretty sharing of mine." Being open with your employees, she believes, means that nothing is a surprise to them - even if you fire them. - Sheryl Sandberg, COO of Facebook[i]

Secondly, because it is a nice way to explain how I gathered my learning and came about my way of working with organisations.

My story starts with a choice my grandfather made once Holland became occupied by the Germans: he joined the Waffen SS, was one of the last to leave Stalingrad, in the wake of it became an officer and was interned after the war.

This had a profound effect on my father: he did not have a role model for being a man and a father, he had a complicated relationship with his own father and he chose early in life that he would make up for the sins of his father. He did so by becoming a career officer in the police and generally working very hard to provide for his family. He was also very restless and always looking for the next challenge. He went on to be a successful intrapreneur and later in life joining central government again as he felt that being an entrepreneur was not relevant enough to impact society.

As a result I spent a very long time looking for a connection with my father. I was a wordy, heady boy, with a deep curiosity for concepts and theories from a young age. It set me apart and I got bullied a lot in secondary school. I thought I was there to finally really start learning something and learnt the hard way that that is of course not the primary objective of attending school.

In my drive to connect to my father, I suppose I took up an early interest in business. My parents always generously supported me in following my curiosity. When I was fourteen, they gave me "Ogilvy on Advertising" which had just come out at that time. It mentioned David's address in one of the best recruitment ads I ever saw. I sent him a letter with some questions. He responded, with answers and a classic D.O. line, curt and incisive: "I do not believe you are only fourteen. Here are my answers to your questions anyway. Please send me a photograph of yourself."

I did. It was the start of a friendship that lasted until he sadly faded away as a result of Alzheimer's. I am forever in his debt for teaching me many things that I am only now beginning to see the true value of, letting me sit in on conversations with some of the leading CEOs of that time and most importantly, taking me under his wings when I was at my most awkward and seeing me for what I could become.

I learnt a lot from my mother. She is a staunch feminist, so come my thirteenth birthday, I was handed a wallet and notified that from now on I was old enough to go shopping and cook at least once a week and that making beds and ironing shirts was now my own responsibility. What I think I am most grateful for to both my parents, but my mother in particular, is that they taught me it pays to stand for something, that you should treat all people on the basis of equality – there is so much beauty in difference (I vividly remember being taken to have tea with the local imam) – and to be independent and curious in all aspects of life.

As I became older, my relationship with my father improved. He mischievously laid the foundations for what I would become when I grew up: a systems thinker and someone with a deep drive to understand human behaviour. We developed a monthly ritual: at the beginning of every month he would bring home huge stacks of matrix-printed sheets with data (that dates me), hand me a pencil and a yellow marker and say simply: "Spot the anomalies". Then we would discuss those and it would morph in to an often passionate dialogue on patterns, analysis and how "following the paper trail" always lays bare the dysfunctional patterns in organisations.

We finally really connected when I was seventeen because he was taking an executive education program in which Manfred Kets de Vries taught that went by the quaint name "Management of Irrational and Dysfunctional Processes in Organisations". In immersing myself in the materials, in subsequent conversation with him, we found a common language. He told me his story and was at last able to tell me why he had always been so aloof and disconnected.

The by-product of that process was that it instilled in me a lifelong fascination with human behaviour and how this is either functional or often dysfunctional in organisations and groups of people. It also helped me crack the code for myself for the first time. When I switched classes, we went on a boot camp. The food our teachers cooked was abysmal so I revolted with some girls and we took over shopping and cooking the next day, to applause from the group. So overnight I went from being an outsider to being a leader, by standing up, connecting and changing my behaviour. This was reinforced further when we evaluated a few weeks later. I spotted two very unhappy, crying girls, who were being bullied. I called the guy who did it on it, told my own story of being bullied and explained him that if he wanted to be very miserable for the next two years he should by all means continue. From then on, the only people who were miserable occasionally were our teachers, because we had become such a close-knit group.

I went to Rotterdam to study. I had spent most of my vacations from my sixteenth working for my uncle's company, a logistics business, being allowed to look deep into the kitchen and given a lot of space to help him make improvements. I had some catching up to do after four out of six years being bullied. I made friends for life and partied more. I dropped out when I was twenty-one. I worked for my uncle and someone gave me the opportunity to start my own business when I was twenty-four. While it was reasonably successful, I decided to close it down after two years. Moving boxes around the world was not my passion, solving tough problems for customers was. There wasn't a viable economic model for that in that business.

I spent the next six years in the IT industry, lastly as second in command of a business that had grown steeply in the preceding years. That's where I learnt the hard way how implementing change works and doesn't work.

Here I also picked up my education again.

In the early nineties, a few people and leading organisations created the MIT Center for Organizational Learning, which later became the Society for Organizational Learning. I have been fortunate to study and collaborate with some of the leading people behind this school of thought. I am particularly fortunate and grateful to have Dr. David Kantor as mentor and friend, who has paved the way on so many domains for me to use his psychotherapeutic body of work of a lifetime in the real context of teams.

As things sometimes go, you find that you cannot apply what you have learnt in the organisation where you work. I set up my consulting business in 2001, which today goes by the name of why* consulting.

While in many ways I stand on the shoulders of David Kantor, Bill Isaacs, Peter Garrett, Peter Senge and Otto Scharmer and many of the concepts and theories you come across are theirs, what I do take credit for is developing a coherent, rigorous methodology out of these that delivers results in organisations and is very practically applicable and easy to understand.

One of my proudest moments is standing on a hilltop in a forest and just watching electricians we had trained explain each other the dynamics in their team in common language and teaching each other to work with it.

Where our approach differentiates itself is that in our practice, we truly integrate the hard stuff and the harder stuff. The hard stuff is about the numbers, the harder stuff would be the "soft" stuff in other people's books, but it's much harder for most of us, as somebody at Shell once taught me. Moreover, we embed it at the level of teams throughout organisations because we believe and have seen in action that they are the key levers for really cracking the code.

Lastly, I have been studying some of the most advanced approaches to psychotherapy and have qualified as a psychotherapist in the process in the last two and a half years. Prompter for this was that I nearly wrecked my marriage following my shadows. It shows up in the work we do with organisations, teams and individuals in that we create experiences for people that allow them to deeply embody new capabilities after they learn them, rather than superficially teaching tips & tricks. We also work with people's personal stories to show them how these can help them and how they get in their own way.

The book sets out to describe some areas where we often find common causes for failure, such as strategy, context and ingrained cultural patterns. It then gives an outline for how you could create a process that breaks that mould and hopefully provocative tasters of the crafts that you can learn to apply them in your own organisation.

I write "crafts" on purpose because they are just that. They should be studied and practiced. They do not offer a single magic button. Sorry. I am still looking for that one myself as well. You will however find simple condensations of these crafts throughout the book that you can experiment with. They're marked out as **Craft # n.**

They are hard work, sometimes frustratingly so, but applying one or all of them in your day-to-day (business) life will start a process of improvement immediately, if you stick to them.

Acknowledgements

I am deeply grateful to my wife Gwen for giving me the space to write this and thus bearing the full weight of the care for three wonderful but rather demanding kids of five and under while I walked around sunny London and hung out there, writing the bulk of this text. I want to say thank you to my clients for putting their trust in me, giving us the opportunity of learning and improving together, even if they might have felt sometimes that what we do is quaint. Or as one of them put it – and I wear it as a badge of honour- when he introduced me to a client of his: "This is Martijn. He's a consultant, but not a typical one. Sometimes it seems outright weird. But in the end he always gets great results."

Also: a deep bow of gratitude to the people at Ground Operations at Schiphol Airport. On returning from London I left my laptop with the latest version in the seat pocket of the airplane. They found it and returned it.

"The way to motivate people is to:

- set high standards (including clear goals)
- recognize excellence
- remove organizational obstacles
- model high-integrity behaviour
- get out of the way

People want the freedom and support to prove their own greatness. And they want to feel like their work matters. No one wants to be a cog in a machine."

Paul King, software entrepreneur, in response to a question on Quora.

"You cannot solve a problem with the same thinking that created it." - Albert Einstein

Problems

Fragmentation

Ever since Descartes tried his hand at modern-day sense-making, we have strayed away from looking at our world as one whole, in which we are all included. Now, if we want to make sense of something, we try to break it down in neat little bits and almost seem to strive to make our approach as mechanistic and technologically advanced and numerically correct and measurable as we can.

When we fail to crack the code, we'll fragment the problem a little further and expect to understand it. The problem is this rarely leads to the sustainable solution we say we are looking for. In doing this, we forget that we are all part of one big (the planet) and several smaller whole systems (our family, the organisations we work in).

Think of human gestation. Even though we are now able to manipulate conception and possibly even what is conceived at that moment, it still boils down to an egg and some semen. These two came about from two other human beings; who in turn sprouted from four others and so on. And each egg, and usually, one lucky spermatozoid are made up out of an almost infinite number of characteristics that in the end are so small in their individual make up, that in the end they still remain too large for us to really understand them. Whether an embryo grows to become a child is dependant on many factors that influence its growth or, in other cases stop this growth.

An even more blunt comparison: in companies we often reorganise by eradicating 10% of the work force or eliminating whole departments.

From a whole systems perspective, that's akin to amputating a limb without too much diagnosis, giving the patient no time to recuperate and expecting him to function better than before.

What this yields at an operational level is blacked-out Outlook calendars and lots of busy time that is (un)surprisingly disconnected from the results people say they want to achieve together.

Stacking

Organizations have tendency to stack. Stacking initiatives, stacking KPIs, stacking processes.

Start asking questions like: "Why are we doing this?" again, also at the nitty-gritty level.

An example: I was facilitating a workshop for a senior European leadership team. One of the topics was the reporting structure. The team concluded, even complained, about how much time it took them every month to produce management reports. I asked them how much time. They answered about 3 to 4 days a month, producing 32 pages of very solid data and analysis.

Then I asked their group president whether he read it and whether it served his purposes. He answered no.

Later, I got the opportunity to work with some on the ground industry sales teams and asked the same questions. It came out that an account manager or business development manager spent about 3 days per week on things related to internal reports and, as a consequence, only two days per week at the customer.

We started working to reconfigure this, simplifying the structure and reducing the amount of time spent on it.

To simplify: it is tempting to add another thing or project to your to do list and much harder to make a "stop doing list". This is an example of what became a strategic lever in this specific context, because in the end the process yielded a lighter version that catered to serve as a yardstick to measure whether the organization was on target and a deeper understanding of the business' dynamics, without the loss of customer facing time.

You have to look one or several layers deeper though. Said one executive after a lot of probing: "I have a real problem here. I can't kill projects. You see, right next to the Dead Projects Graveyard is the Dead Project Leaders Graveyard." How you define failure and deal with how it's perceived can cause a major shift in your effectiveness. If you initiate something at the top, be mindful of how it compounds down the road and will bog down what you are actually trying to achieve.

Sometimes you need to slow down to go faster

Some people call it the Whirlwind[ii]. I have often described it as The Parallel Universe or the Big White Void. What it describes is what happens most of the time when you make plans to change something in an organisation: you detail what it is, communicate it in a workshop or town hall session and then, to a large extent, it falls flat on its face.

People often understand that something needs to change and are of good will to make it happen. And then they get sucked into the Big White Void of daily corporate life. All the daily stuff that keeps them off the street. As result, some 70% of change efforts fail.

Generating lasting change is a craft that needs to be learnt. This takes time and a different sense of time. The ancient Greeks distinguished *chronos* and *kairos*. The first is chronological time; the second was used to define a space and time where special things can emerge.

Rather than weekly conference calls, team meetings, "bilaterals", scrum sessions and what have you, invest in bringing the people that are instrumental to deliver your goals together for two to three days per quarter. Hang out. If you make time for this and attach a good process to it, what needs to happen becomes almost self-evident and self-fulfilling. The further goods news is that, to borrow a beautiful metaphor from Robert Quinn, you can build the bridge while your walking on it, thus avoiding your initiative getting sucked into the Void.

When back in *chronos,* the Outlook calendars become filled with things that will actually deliver the results you are looking for and mailboxes stop overflowing with what is mostly cover-your-ass crap and verbal drivel.

Cracking The Code

Organisations, why bother?

Even though or when there is an economic downturn, I believe change has become a constant - if it ever wasn't. After 9/11 I see that a lot of the action and policies governments and organisations make are driven by fear and often, just plain regression. In keeping with what I know about how perception often works - failing to see where really you are, because you are part of the system you are trying to influence or describe and by that very nature, can rarely see from the outside in - any focus on developing new ways of organising currently gets a lot of pushback. Everybody reverts back to the command-and-control model as the best modus operandi again.

Yet I think we are in urgent need of new ways of organising. Our current systems for running companies and managing people, money and work (and our lives, for that matter) are not helpful towards making this world a better place, let alone making most individual people happy, or for that matter, producing above average returns.

Much of the systems we keep alive together are based on control, reproduction and rigid frameworks.

A lot of what would help, in my view, is paradoxically about letting go, creativity, change and dynamic processes. Wouldn't it be nice if we could redefine the (corporate) landscape to tap in to this?

I think:

- The best people will not continue to work for organisations if they do not have the feeling that what they do there 8+ hours a day contributes fundamentally to their personal growth/happiness. (Not wealth, primarily)

- Good people will increasingly look for environments where they can be who they really are instead of performing in a role as specified top down for them. (Self-actualisation vs. providing)

- Each individual will want an individual package that suits their personal needs. Otherwise they will work somewhere else or find a way to break out of the system. (Or the system will drive them out, with all its unpleasant consequences)

- Even if the economy in the developed world suffers further setbacks, the generic level of wealth is so high and the demand for skilled workers so big, that the best "employees" will increasingly set the agenda for negotiations. "Why am I doing this?" and "What's in it for me? (Not just in terms of money) will remain key questions in the years to come.

- Being given the opportunity to lead is a core driver for people, money isn't necessarily[iii]:

Exhibit

It's not about the money

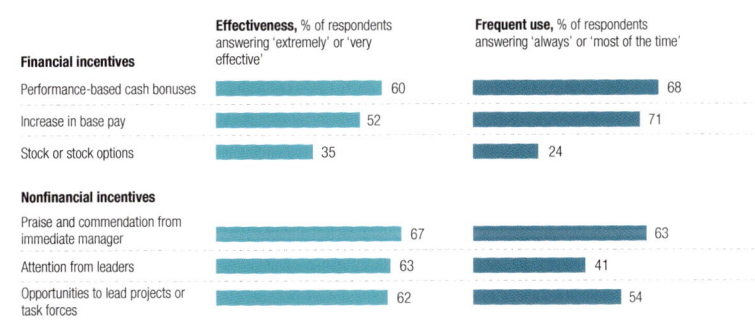

- I see several C-level and senior executives rolling their eyes and hear you grind you teeth: they should adapt to our frameworks and adhere to my policies! Err… Individuals that are better developed and get the space to show up as who they are simply deliver better results to your company. They just don't like being regimented. Why do you think Gen Y-ers and Millenials like working for Facebook or Google? How does your EBIT compare to theirs? And your share price?

- Moreover, the pressure to do more, faster, with less resources will only increase. If you want to achieve this from a command & control perspective, you will fail.

If companies want to be sustainable in the long run, I feel that if you are a "manager", you are going to have to set "employees" free. You should provoke them to think for themselves and speak their minds. You should stimulate them to look for who they really are and what they really want and to make a meaningful contribution from that starting point. You should try and let go of a lot of things.

If you want other people to be open, you are asking them to be vulnerable. They are never going to do that if you are not prepared to do just that yourself. Which implies you will have to make a big decision – my take, with your heart, not your head - to start accepting everybody as they are and treating them on the basis of equality. This is complicated and of course you are going to meet resistance, starting with your own.

BIG IDEA:

Limits to organisational survival will increasingly be set by the extent to which an organisation is able to distribute to and develop leadership at all layers of an organisation.

In essence, we will need everybody to bring their best leadership, from the boardroom to the mailroom, every day.

This calls for a fundamental shift in how we define leadership and its development.

Perhaps paradoxically, it will require the most from senior leaders.

It may be that David Ogilvy was –again– prescient when he compared his role with that of a constitutional monarch in Bagehot's definition: *"The right to be consulted, the right to encourage and the right to warn."*

Impeding convictions

Let's assume you are anywhere between 25 and 60.

Has it ever occurred to you that from the day you went to elementary school, implicitly or explicitly, efforts have been made to make you comply, reproduce what others had reproduced before you and think along lines that haven't changed fundamentally for years/ages/centuries?

Not to mention the way you can slide off in most organisations, because these systems seek your compliance, rather than your commitment. Compliance seemingly leads to control, which apparently remains the underlying objective of organisations. In the mental model of many organisations, commitment is actually not a good thing, because that leads to overt displays of individualism, which would lead to loss of control.

Implications for organising work

I feel traditional hierarchies are or should become a thing of the past. I have a few reasons for that. One: they impede creative exploration and the rapid innovation that follows from it. Experts as well as most CEOs[iv] seem to agree rationally that the latter is the only true competitive edge for organisations in the next years. I do not however, see the change needed happening in terms of organisational design, mind-set and behaviours in many organisations. I do believe that it will in the long run be identified as an economic necessity for the survival of companies. And that has always proved to be a powerful catalyst for change.

Another one: because people are increasingly aware of their own potential, both intellectually as well as spiritually, I plainly see it as an insult to their intelligence to constrain them in strong hierarchies and I suspect they themselves will perceive it as such, if this assumption proves to be true.

My definition of an organisation is:

A group of people that work together to achieve joint and personal objectives.

Why that broad? Because in my view, with the pace at which business is conducted, the (legal) form is loosing relevance to the practical applicability of ways to operate. Eventually, I hope companies will be born, merged, acquired and disbanded at the same speed as the circumstances or people's objectives dictate. I do hope that groups of people that have fun working with each other and get a sense of accomplishment from what they're doing will stick together. What becomes interesting to explore in the time to come, are the protocols that enable these people to work together effectively towards attaining the goals they have set themselves with the objective of doing that as smoothly and efficiently as they can.

If there is a structure, it should be flat, with short lines of communication. "Yeah right", you'll say, "we heard that before." Very true, but have you ever seen many where they *actually* work like that? If there is a structure, it should also be flexible. People have unique personal capabilities, which should be the starting point of organising work, rather than one special trick someone has learnt to play somewhere along the road.

If you take capabilities as a starting point, there's another added bonus. Capability centric organisation leads a group of people to know what the individual competencies of each individual are, which in turn allows the group to organize themselves in a much more cyclical way, treating each challenge as a project, staffing it jointly based on its desired output rather than on the politically correct input.

In short, it should enable people to contribute their best and to grow to achieve specific, clear objectives that serve the organisation as a whole and the world around it.

What purpose does organisation serve than, based on these thoughts?

Roles for organisations

In my view it can fulfil the following roles:

- Facilitator
- Motivator/coach
- Broker/clearing house
- Body of Knowledge

Facilitator:

A theme that fascinates me is *economies of scale*. It does so because we live in a capitalist society, the longest surviving working model (with a moderate degree of happiness for the majority of people in the Western world, I mean) to date, and as a driver, it remains one of the most powerful and convincing arguments for organising yourself in a group rather than doing it all by yourself.

In conjunction with this, facilitator of economies of scales came up, mainly on the cost side of turnover. In a broader sense, it should also facilitate learning or the exchange of value and values.

Why am I pushing this latter term? Because it differs radically from our classical perception of the organisation: the management as the regulating body at the top, with the employees as "directable" and "changeable" in a direction that best serves the latest whim or is most in line with the latest management fad, with a distribution of wealth that is based on seniority rather than merit.

Motivator/coach:

Whether this is something a whole organisation can do I am not sure, but it does touch on something I think is another reason that makes it valid to organise: furthering individual and collective learning.

The risk in doing that, is that it could be based too strongly on traditional models as well. I make the case here for values that in my view are imperative for true, deep learning: respect, treating all people on the basis of equality and real collaboration.

The work that has taken shape around Peter Senge[v] and evolved from Kolb's thinking[vi] on (team) learning styles corroborates the necessity to take into consideration that if each individual has a different style of learning, this in turn means that if you have collective true learning as an objective, you must find ways to incorporate the aforementioned values when building a system for obtaining this learning. In my view, true learning incorporates the master teaching the younger the skills of a trade as much as the younger who questions the elders to further his learning as well as *theirs*. As a rabbi once said: "I thank the great wise men of all ages, for I have learnt a lot from them. I thank my teachers, for I have learnt even more from them. I owe the greatest debt of gratitude to my students, for I have learnt by the most from them." I feel that if a group of people are able to organise this together, this can be one of the most powerful qualifiers for an existence as an organisation.

Broker/clearing house:

As mentioned earlier, companies in the traditional sense seem to be losing in importance. I pondered on the implications of organisations becoming part of global networks increasingly. This led me to draw the analogy with computer networks.

I feel that the Internet -as a Platonic idea- is successful because it is the only really true open and global network. It operates entirely on a set of protocols that share a few strong starting points that I now feel might also hold out well in a living system (organisation), not in the least because the Internet *is* a living system.

These protocols:

- Are universally accepted (to the extent that this achievable), because they are created *through* the community that uses them and not exclusively by a top heavy standards committee;
- Are designed to achieve optimum efficiency and ease of processing between a wide range of users, with very different characteristics, but generically they strive for inclusion and

accommodation of all varieties of users, rather than on "some are more equals than others" standards;
- Are regularly reviewed on quality, ease of use and relevance;
- Are abolished or transformed when no longer appropriate.

The conditions you can read through these lines in my view are perpendicular to the way companies and organisations work in most cases. Furthermore, an inordinate amount of time, energy and money gets lost in making shared objectives fit in a system that is generically not cut out to just that. The existing system starts from an altogether different paradigm: advocacy. Organisation vs. employee. Legal party #1 vs. Legal party #2 (perish the thought if you would want to include # 3 and #4). Such a systemic perspective strives for exclusion, rather than inclusion and take out a lot of speed from getting things going or done.

This has brought me to the idea that you have a valuable proposition towards people and other organisations when you enable them, and therewith yourself, to increase the speed and efficiency they do their own unique thing with. An organisation can do this by offering them a framework and readymade protocols and invite them to help shape these protocols in the future.

In keeping with this idea, an organisation can act as a broker between people doing their own unique thing and as a clearing house (including all the administrative stuff, which happens to be the unique thing some people enjoy doing as well) for the results of the execution of these protocols.

KNOWLEDGE PER SE IS OBSOLETE. THE POWER TO AGGREGATE IT EFFECTIVELY TAKES OVER.

Body of knowledge:

Any organisation is, per se, a body of knowledge, because in more or less effective ways it is a collective of intelligent human beings. What is interesting for me, is whether you can consciously take action to achieve what so many textbooks on knowledge management hint on, but fail to name or really achieve because their models exclude too much:

How can we create a form of true collective intelligence or at least endeavour to tap in to that?

In my exploration with other people and clients around a new type of organisation we are trying to find, we have so far seen results with trying to build on a form of collective intelligence because we decided to do things very differently.

In any case, it involves a true love of exploration and the willingness to suspend assumptions in the participants.

How I'd visualise this is as follows:

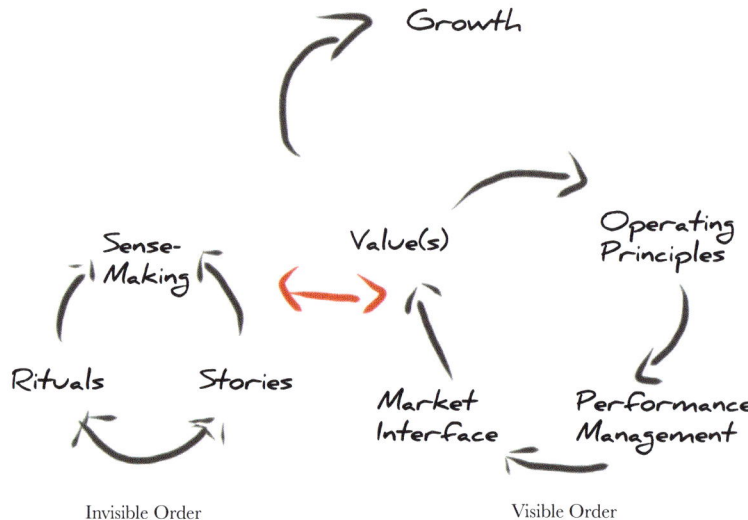

Invisible order

If there is a group of people and they want to do something or be together, there are three things that play a crucial role and are always present in a functional or dysfunctional way:

> *Sense making, rituals and stories.*

These were there as long as we have had the gift of being able to hand them on to future generations and anything we do in groups can still be categorised under at least one of them.

If it is not working out between them, there are many reasons, but often they concentrate around the following themes:

- They do not know what their purpose is or are pursuing different/the wrong ones
- They do not have enough awareness of their rituals, they have strayed away from what works, or they do not honour them.
- They have stopped telling each other stories that convey power/action, meaning or affect.

One of the things I want to demonstrate in this book is the value of an on-going dialogue process in the workplace and its relationships.

In fostering that, an organisation makes space for sense-making, rituals and story, all of which are fundamental needs of the human spirit. These needs find ways to be met without formal dialogue- through gossip, departmental celebrations, dress down days, ritualised trips to the coffee machine and many other ways.

However, the introduction of space for real dialogue enables stories to be surfaced and validated or otherwise given meaning. It ensures time to make sense of changes. It provides a place for creative ideas to be considered and developed. The value to the organisation is healing of the losses involved in change and harnessing energy that is released when people realise their connection to each other and renew their commitment to their work.

It is easy to stop exploring your true drivers collectively -because all seems to be going well or you are caught in the Big White Void- that I am beginning to feel that if there is one capability that is worth embedding deeply in an organisation, it is this.[vii]

Visible order

Shared values can be translated into operating principles, encompassing strategy, which are either protocols for doing business or thoughts and 'rules' about how to go about doing business. In order to create or maintain sustainability, you will have to agree on some form of performance management, which is not a role or a function as much as it is a shared responsibility. If you are a profit & loss based organisation, you are going to need a form of a market interface to interact with the market you choose to operate in. Following through to the last arrow, in engaging in these activities, you create value. For yourself and for your customers, who give you feedback or pushback in the form of money, interaction and by expressing their content or discontent with what you supply or create with them jointly.

My thinking on the increasing importance of space for individuals to bring their whole self to work, leads me to the perhaps easy or contestable conclusion that if there is any reason to still pursue that in a group of people rather than on your own, it is because you share values and a common purpose.

Somewhere in this soup, people start turning out great stuff. Ultimate example: Semco in Brazil, consistently for the last 40 years. Check it out. More recent example: Tony Hsieh's tale of redemption at Zappos.com. His core message is about happiness and Zappos.com deliver that.

It's contagious, as my blog post from a few years back shows:

"A while ago, I came across this funny company called zappos.com. It's interesting, because they don't even formally trade in Holland. Yet I found the tweets that its CEO, Tony Hsieh posted so funny, weird and interesting that I researched it. So I asked for their culture book. And sure enough, this wasn't a fad, within 5 working days - Vegas to Holland, that's 5400 miles for you- the UPS guy was on my doorstep. So there was the first WOW experience.

Then I learned that Tony was about to publish a book. And that I could get a free advance copy if committed to review it. Again within a heartbeat, the UPS guy rings the bell at the office door. I get not one but two copies, with all sorts of smart thinking about how to entice me to spread the word. WOW experience #2.

I am an advisor that helps organizations transform their way of working together and build healthy cultures. So I am running a program for client where I think a dialogue with Tony would help them a lot. I send him a message. I am contacted within 24 hours with precisely the right information by his European representative. WOW experience #3.

Why am I sharing all of this with you? Because its easy to SAY that you deliver happiness. But at Zappos they DO it every day. The aforementioned three instances show that pretty conclusively for me.

So I can write a long, semi-scientific review of Tony's book. Or I can tell you that you should buy it. Because his story is worth reading. It's a story of how he sold his first company for $ 265 million. And that running that company made him wretchedly unhappy. And how he invested in Zappos, became its CEO and nearly "blew" all the money he made in life on it. Why? Because he passionately believed (and believes) that you could run a company in a different and healthy way. Where people actually are...happy. And what's more, make their stakeholders happy as its core offering. For the skeptics: it grew from 0 to $ 1 billion in revenues in under 10 years. It was sold to Amazon in the first ever stock only deal they did for $ 1.2 billion at the time of closing. And they promised they wouldn't change the culture.

While the book is not a how-to guide and at some points lacks structure for the more traditionally oriented, it's a story worth reading and if you digest it properly, there's a ton you can learn from these people."

It is easy to stop exploring your true drivers collectively -because all seems to be going well or you are caught in the Big White Void- that I am beginning to feel that if there is one thing that is worth institutionalising in an organisation, it is this.[viii]

> BEFORE YOU CAN SEE WHERE YOU NEED TO GO, YOU NEED TO KNOW WHERE YOU REALLY ARE.

Taking stock

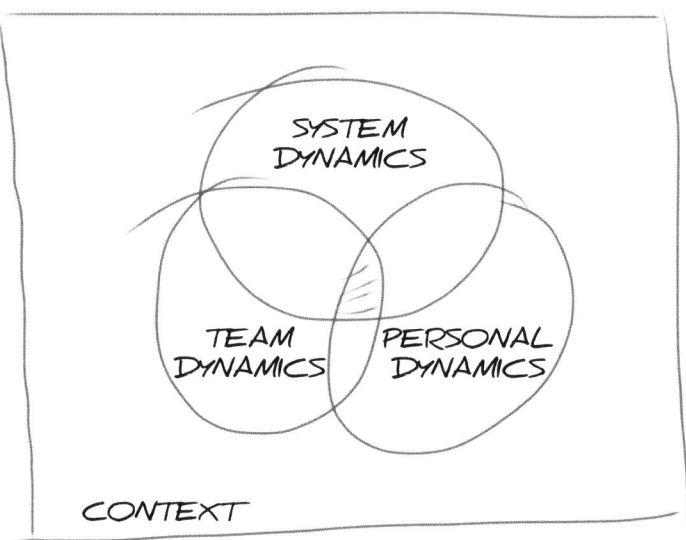

To the best of my knowledge, there aren't many models that integrate the "hard" and "soft" aspects of organisation in diagnosis and provide practical underlying tools to coherent systemic interventions.

The above does and has worked for some 25,000 people[ix] in some way, shape or form in the last 7 years.

The essence of it is that there are always four types of **dynamics** that play a role in how an organisation operates with more or less success:

- **Context(ual) dynamics**– represented by the rectangle, which is often neglected: we all think we know in which context we work, but rarely tend to make it explicit in conversation. As a result we frequently lack awareness of the internal and external *constraints*[x] this context imposes upon us as a team or an organisation.

- **System dynamics**– an organisation can be diagnosed and intervened upon as a system. While it seems close to impossible to objectively gauge your own organisation from the outside in, looking at it through a whole system lens is as close as you can get if you do it collectively. Closely tied to the context.

- **Team dynamics–** we go to school and university and learn many things, but rarely how things work between people or rather, don't. Through learning a codified, uniform language of observable human behaviour, you can identify blind spots and dramatically improve raise self-awareness and interaction in teams. This in turn boosts performance. Automatic by-product: much more fun and happiness.

- **Personal dynamics–**

    "I believe in bringing your whole self to work. We are who we are. When you try to have this division between your personal self and professional self, what you really are is stiff…" - Sheryl Sandberg.

    I could hardly say it better, which is why I repeat it again here. Maybe a few defining words on "stiff": not fully there, not delivering on your full potential as a human being, incongruent, unsure-footed, uncomfortable, out of place. Your individual story and that of your colleagues play a major role in how you show up every day, particularly when the stakes get high. If you can own the highs and lows of that, things simply tend to flow more naturally for you.

For each of these areas, there are practical tools that serve to diagnose, form hypotheses and intervene. I will explore them more fundamentally with you as we mosey along through this book.

The key however is that following this methodology, you can always come up with one to three **strategic levers** that you will find somewhere on the intersection of these four areas. They are likely to work on all four areas simultaneously when implemented. They also seem pretty obvious once you find them. And they're likely to be an answer to the question: "What's the smallest thing you can do to make the biggest impact?

Pricing system

In a workshop with an industry sales team, we found that the way they priced their products was inadequate. On top of that, the system for getting clearance for quoting to a customer wasn't working, in that they were losing business due to its complexity and slowness. Because the group came together as a team, they really saw this problem. Because a shift happened for them personally, they found the courage to discuss it openly with a senior manager we had invited for dinner that night (by design, because I knew from experience that this kind of stuff comes up). Because the context and their understanding of it was different, they could present the problem confidently and concisely. As a result, they were asked to come up with one single sheet of paper to describe the problem and a solution. This was adopted and implemented in the space of a month for the whole organisation.

Risk management circle

While we were hosting a workshop for the risk management team of a financial institution a market position problem arose that needed to be addressed on the spot. They gathered in a circle, standing up, as a team. I stood by. When they were done discussing the problem, I asked simply: "How often do you do this, like this?" The answer came immediately from the CRO: "Too little." "We don't have a space for doing it" said another team member. "How could you create a space?" "By clearing a room and I am happy to give my room for it" said the second in command. "You and I need to spend more time together, because we do not communicate well and often enough, I realised as a result of this workshop, so I want you to set up your desk in my room" said the CRO. A meaningful silence ensued. "We'll create a room with just some standing tables and a huge black board or white board. That's how we'll do our team meetings from now on." "Yes!" said most team members with a smile on their face.

This is where you start to crack your code.

Dialogue

Before we can launch into diagnosis, we need to address something that in fact determines the outcome of everything else: the quality of our conversations and thus, our collective thinking.

In the late seventies and early eighties, the theoretical physicist David Bohm was running conversations with his Ph. D students and later, several other interested people. As you may know, theoretical physicists tend to be highly conceptual people who are always looking to understand and explain the order of things. Generalising, they are fascinated by such things as:

- Energy
- Space
- Fields
- Time

In the wake of these conversations, they discovered that conversations in an implicit way are also influenced or even governed by the concepts listed above. The model you see depicted here was developed from those conversations.[xi]

"Dialogue" comes from the Old Greek and finds its roots in *dialogos*. "Flow of meaning" is its translation. The core of dialogue is inquiry. That inquiry surfaces ideas, perceptions, and understanding that people do not already have. This is not the usual norm: we typically try to come to important conversations well prepared. A hallmark for many of us is that there are "no surprises" in our meetings. Yet this is perpendicular to having a dialogue. You have a dialogue when you explore the uncertainties and questions that no one has answers to. In this way you begin to *think together*- not simply report out loud old thoughts. In dialogue you learn to use the energy of differences to enhance and connect to collective wisdom.

Dialogue can be contrasted with "discussion", a word whose roots mean "to break apart". Discussions are conversations where people hold onto and defend their differences. The hope is that the clash of opinions will lead to a productive road to action and insight.

In practice, discussion often ends in rigid debate (coming, literally, from "to beat down") where people view each other as positions to agree with or refute. They are their point of view rather than having one. Such exchanges create a series of one-way streets, and the end results are often not what people wish for: heated arguments where people withhold vital information and shut down.

Below, you see how a conversation can evolve into a dialogue. Or not. There are four stages: **Politeness, Breakdown, Inquiry & Flow.**

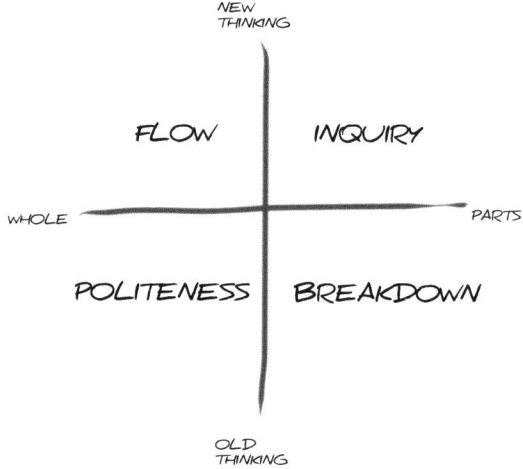

If you create the time and right space, you can learn to see what kind of energy is present in each of these fields.

Most conversations in life do not go beyond breakdown and revert back to politeness. I have often dubbed this the Politeness Roundabout. If it happens often, it starts to feel cold, stale and disingenuous. But it is also profoundly human: we are at ease when things are whole and seemingly comfortable. Being in breakdown means we have to show our true colours or, if the pressure is high enough, cannot help ourselves stepping into our shadows, so breaking down in parts. The pattern of moving from politeness to breakdown and then quickly back to politeness leads us to perpetuate old thinking.

How to recognize this? At its worst, the response of a chairperson after a heated exchange between two members of a group has taken place:

"Well...eur... Under the circumstances it seems best if we move that topic to the next meeting and continue with the agenda now...."

And everybody files in and agrees and the meeting moves on. Without the real issues having been touched on. Or a discussion with a life partner that ends with one of you shouting: "Fine!" and leaving the room. Which is of course about as far from "fine" as you can be.

In more subtle terms, it's where one of your team members does something out of the ordinary, which surprises other team members and a slightly uncomfortable silence ensues. Or a new boss steps in and everybody takes a polite wait & see attitude in the first two meetings, so they in effect become one-way traffic.

But you can learn to break that pattern, if you learn *to hold the heat* together in breakdown.

There are two things that help: understanding how dynamics in the team or group you are part of work and experimenting with different behaviours.

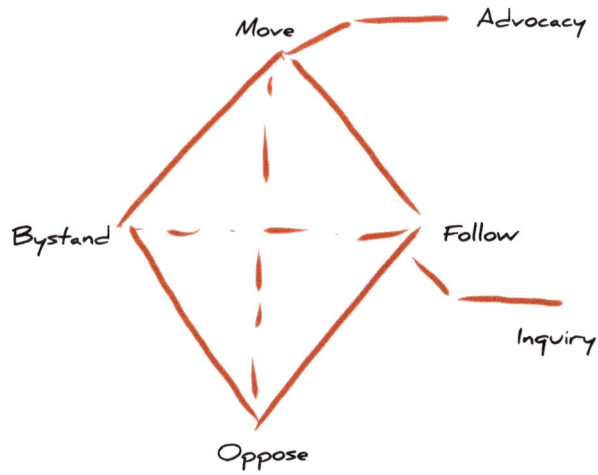

We'll cover this in more detail in the section about Teams, but in any given group of people, there are people who naturally move, people who follow, people that oppose and people that bystand. In a healthy team, these energies are present in a balanced way. Why? Without movers, there's no *initiative*. Without followers there's no *completion*. Without opposers, there's no *correction*. Without bystanders, there's no *perspective*.

There are capabilities associated with each of these four energies:

MOVE *Voicing* - to speak from your own true voice, defined as being moved to speak and express what needs to be said at a particular moment. This requires internal monitoring to check that voicing is about more than feeling pressured to speak or about being motivated by desires for attention. True voicing may feel that the words come from somewhere beyond yourself.

FOLLOW *Listening*- attentively, by letting go of opinions and ideas. True listening enables common understanding and the resolution of differences. Acquiring the internal stillness to listen is not easy for people from western cultures.

OPPOSE *Respecting*- involves looking for the best in a person, honouring their boundaries and not discounting their view. Respect requires inquiry not imposition, understanding not judgement.

BYSTAND *Suspending*- is about observing thoughts and feelings but not necessarily acting on them. It is about waiting and not moving towards premature closure. Suspending requires that we learn to accept uncertainty. It is also about trying to see what is happening as an object that you can look at, walk around, inspect and then say what you see, without judging it.

How can you work with this? Practice. Instead of reacting straight away, ask for a pause. Take a breath. Exhale. Tell what you feel. Take a different position. Inquire. For example: instead of saying: "I disagree with that!" ask: "Why do you want to do it that way? Please tell me more." Instead of saying: "I want it done. Now." explain why it's important to you. When you're getting into a debate that looks all too familiar, say: "I think we're sliding off to where we don't want to be. What can I do to change that?" When you are listening, but find your attention waning, say: "I notice I am having difficulty following you. Could you try to rephrase it."

You'll also note in the diagram that move-oppose represents the line of *advocacy*. Bystand-follow represents the line of *inquiry*. Put simply, advocacy shows up in a conversation as statements, inquiry in the form of questions.

There's conclusive research[xii] that neither more advocacy nor inquiry create better performing teams.

It's the ratio that makes the difference:

	Advocacy	**Inquiry**
Low performance teams	1.0	0.1
High performance teams	1.1	1.0

In other words, low performance teams make roughly 10 statements for every question they ask among themselves, high performance teams virtually alternate between them.

How you can move from breakdown to inquiry easily is through asking questions. Realise that different questions have different impact. How you ask them (tone, intensity, energy) also affects the flow of the conversation.

There's a hierarchy:

Question type:	Impacts/ invites:	Positive	Negative
Why	Identity	Why do we frequently seem to get stuck together on this topic?	Why can you not solve this problem? It's your remit after all.
How	Solution	How could we also look at this problem?	How could you even think this would fly?
What	Inquiry	What is really happening here? Can we look below the waterline for a moment?	What is the solution? I want some answers now.
Who/when/where	Accountability	Who could help us look at this differently?	Who is responsible for this cock up?
Yes/No question	Closure/understanding	Am I correctly rephrasing what you just said when I say…	So you are the one who dropped the ball on this, right?

You'll find that if you invite reflection by asking open questions, when you hit breakdown, a group will actually really be willing most of the time to inquire into what is really going on, because everybody's drive is ultimately to resolve things and make things better. They just have different ways of contributing to that. The space you are looking for is where people can *have* a point of view, rather than *being* their point of view. Sometimes it's messy, but with some practice, it becomes a cornerstone for moving through the four fields quickly and effectively, thus greatly enhancing a team's performance. Once you've seen it work, you want more.

> **Dialogue - How do I stack up?**
>
> - What's the quality of the dialogue in your team and organisation?
> - How's the balance between advocacy and inquiry in our team?
> - What dynamics do we see in our team?
> - How generative are our conversations?
> - How often do we end up on Politeness Roundabout?

Craft # 1 - Dialogue

A simple way to experiment with this is to simply try it out. Pick a topic that you know is important to and has been dangling for a while in your team.

Prepare

Send out an invitation that contains a just a few simple questions and ask people to reflect on these. This ensures people show up attuned to the same purpose and energy. This is 40% of the work. If you have time, interview them individually by just repeating these questions. Listen. Sample questions:

- What gives you energy in our team?
- What makes you loose energy in our team?
- If I could change one thing today, it would be...

Time

Allow generous time for a session. Allocate about two hours. Get something nice to eat. Welcome slowing down.

Space

Look for a space out of the ordinary. A meeting room that is only artificially lit is not a good idea. The beach, a park or a forest are. As is a room with lots of natural light. No tables. Just a neat circle of chairs, please.
"Wvat, no tables?" exclaimed a German client. "Yes, Helmut. No tables."

Check in

Briefly explain the model (page 52) as best as you can. If you are indoors, keep it on a whiteboard or flip chart, so you have a gauge. Contract for space and safety: Please switch off your mobiles. What is said here has a time, a space and a company, so can we agree that what is said here stays here. (Or words of a similar nature)

Ask people to check in, in no particular order, so when they feel moved to speak. Ask them to speak to how they are doing, what they are thinking or feeling. Let the conversation take its course from there.

Energy/fields

Monitor the energy. Where do you think you are in your inner theatre?

- *Politeness*: apprehensive, checked out, going over your shopping list
- *Breakdown*: anxious, angry, agitated, scared, uncomfortable
- *Inquiry*: attentive, eager to contribute, interested, inquisitive
- *Flow*: fully present, moved, happy, touched, quiet, at peace

The rest of the group? What is waiting to happen? What's the balance between advocacy and inquiry?

Check out

For the last 10 minutes or so, check out. Ask simply: "what did we think of this meeting?" and see what learning you can capture. If you just take this into your regular meetings and carry it through with discipline, you'll find that after the initial awkwardness, this is where you end up talking turkey with each other and the quality of your interaction will improve a lot. No unfinished business.

System Dynamics: Framing Systemic Challenges

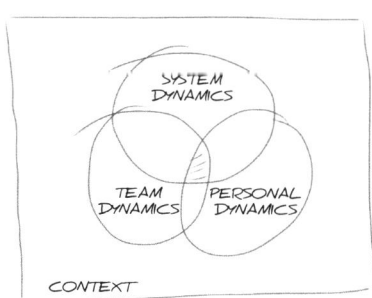

It's incredibly tempting, based on our common frames of reference, to look at diagnosis and bringing about change as a process as depicted in the diagram above. Unfortunately, there is no such thing as LINEAR change. In our simplifications, we do not do credit to the complexity of systems and often as a result, instead of reducing complexity, we increase it, because we come up with one-dimensional solutions.

It's my belief that organisations can solve 80% of their problems, with or without the help of consultants. This however, structurally leaves 20% unaddressed. It's often here that the structural causes of the other 80% can be found. These are often below the waterline, count as non-discussable or as Richard Farson has once beautifully formulated it[xiii]: "Nothing is as invisible as the blindingly obvious."

In not addressing what's below the waterline, we short-change ourselves. People are born as natural systems thinkers. This is why children ask "why?" all the time and are capable to learn more in the first ten years of their lives than most people learn in a lifetime. Because we're also taught to stop questioning things and comply, as I posited earlier.

A lens that may benefit you is my interpretation of Otto Scharmer's Theory U represented in the next diagram. People often think you can bring about change by "taking things from A → B". Stretch the line of the arrow a bit in your mind, chunk it in neat little bits, add some milestones and deliverables and we'll get there. Most of the time, unfortunately, we don't. If you remember a time where you underwent a successful change process, you will inevitably also have gone through a trough of some sort and once you had been there, things started to fall in place and come together.

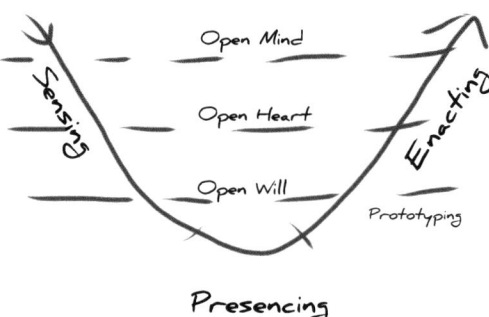

A lot of change processes succeed at accessing people's open mind. So they get it. Less change processes succeed at accessing people's open heart. This provides them with insight and might even move them, but it will not make them move. Only very few approaches to change succeed at mobilising people's open will, which is where they become self-motivated to change and get going.

Design

This is where you'll see the cracks, it's not always a pretty sight and this is also where it is sorely tempting to start fixing. Not yet please. Slow down. I'd like to introduce a different notion of design as formulated by Andrew Pickering:

"A distinctly cybernetic notion of design, very different from that more familiar in modern science and engineering. If our usual notion of design entails the formulation of a plan which is then imposed upon matter, the cybernetic approach entailed instead a continuing interaction with materials, human and non-human, to explore what might be achieved – what one might call an *evolutionary* approach to design, that necessarily entailed a degree of respect for the other.[xiv]"

This is the stance you are looking for. And need to stick to. It's somewhere at the bottom where between letting go and letting come you find the levers to shift the game. That's why I introduced the cybernetic notion of design versus the drive to fix and impose a plan. In keeping with this, you need to tinker with it and prototype the ideas and test them, validate them and for example, need to invite some of the staunchest company critics for a test drive.

If it feels like you are stuck at the bottom of a halfpipe sometimes, you are probably precisely where you need to be.

Somewhere in this process, you will see where things need to go. You can then take the step of developing a few scenarios as to how this could unfold for you.

scenario
/səˈne(ə)rēˌō/

Noun
1. A written outline of a movie, novel, or stage work giving details of the plot and individual scenes.
2. A postulated sequence or development of events.[xv]

Try to craft scenarios from what you found in your exploration. If done well, they foster understanding, create enormous focus and become an invaluable asset in running your business better. Not more than three get released into the organisation. Key ingredients:

Good names – we will either end up with "**Nuclear War**", "**Conventional War with many casualties**" or "**World Peace**". Everybody gets that in one.

Good storyline – a clear descriptive narrative of what will likely happen and what the impact will be for each scenario if it unfolds.

Good metrics - what simple metrics do you apply to filter data to know where you are? (Money/behaviour/events/milestones)

The journey starts, however, with doing a simple collective thinking exercise, presented below as Craft #2.

What continues to amaze me is how easy it is to get people at all levels to start accessing the skill of systems thinking again and how, usually in under two hours, the systemic issues that get in the way of success are on a flip chart, following the next simple exercise[xvi].

Craft #2 – Systems Thinking – What's the Real Problem?

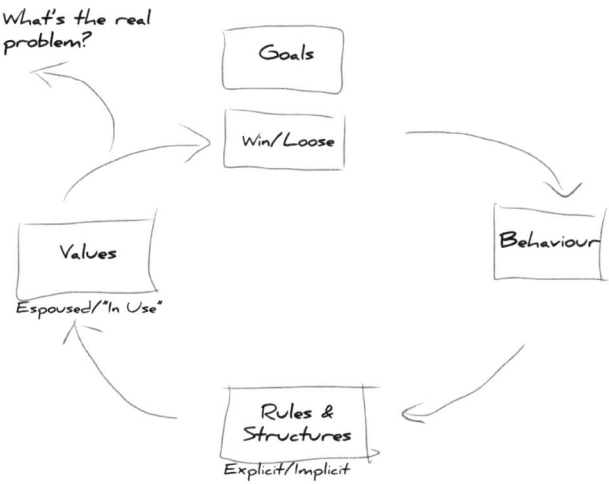

Be it as a team, or as an organisation, we set ourselves goals. We hit some, we miss some. Where we do not succeed is where it gets interesting, because often I find that a wealth of insight can be gained there and structural systemic solutions can be found.

PART I (15" – 60") Problem Definition

- What are goals? Objectives? Challenges? Problems?
- Where are we hitting the mark?
- Where are we missing it?
- Why is this important?

61

- How does this affect our performance?
- What other areas does this affect?
- Are we in **politeness, breakdown or inquiry** in this conversation?
- Which elephants are we not naming?

PART II – Behaviour (15"-30")

- What behaviour are we showing that *rewards* us to keep things the way they are?

PART III – Rules & Structures (15"-30")

- What in our rules & structures *rewards* us to display this behaviour or keep things the way they are?
- **Note**: there are explicit rules (code of conduct, business principles) and implicit rules, like when you float an idea at the water cooler and some says: "that won't fly with John" or you're new in a job and someone says to you after a meeting, as a put down: "That's not how we do things at BFOC!" This is the area where you can literally surface the code if you are courageous and honest.

PART IV – Values (15'-30")

- What is it in our values that *rewards* us to sustain the problem?
- **Note:** there are espoused values (the once you find in the glossy brochures) and values "in use". Quite frequently, there is a gap or even conflict between these. Simplest example: "People, Planet, Profit" (espoused) In use: Profit. Period.

When you conduct this analysis with a good group of people, you will be surprised at the patterns you will uncover. After this, you'll automatically ask each other "So, what is the real problem here?" and can start taking that forward.

Set up:

- Do your homework. Ask people to come prepared and make sure that you have access to all the data to make a session productive. It's surprising how often people for example literally have to look up their annual targets on the fly when I host a session like this.
- Get the right people in the room. If there is some kind of beef with Supply Chain Management, get somebody in the room instead of furthering the dysfunctional "they" – "us" dialectic. Venting is not the objective here. Resolving is. I have seen big issues that had been hanging around for 2 or 3 years in an organisation be resolved in 30 minutes by doing just this many times.
- Get a good room (light, space, air), ditch the tables. Work standing up in front of two flip charts. Take a break at a natural moment. Move. If a group is bigger than 6 people, split up, but stay in the same room. Conduct the same exercise and brief each other at the end. Spot the similarities (No shit, Sherlock...) and explore the differences. Put the model on the chart and appoint one person to doodle along. More is better in this exercise.

System Dynamics: Conditions for success

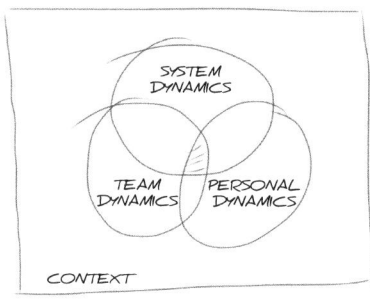

Strategy is underrated.

Not a lot of people get what strategy actually is anymore, because of our culture of fragmenting things, preferably also down to 140 characters. In my mind it's not a vision, it is not a set of goals and it is never vague.

"We want to grow our business from 750 million to 1.5 billion in revenues over the next 3 years."

"We want to be number one in our industry in two years."

'We want to lead the way in sustainable development."

None of these is a strategy. They're objectives.

A good definition of strategy is a *set of carefully crafted rules and measures to overcome specific, complex challenges.*[xvii]

Great organizations find a few -not many- strategic levers to achieve these. They constantly strive to find the smallest thing that will make the biggest impact. (On our four domains: context, system, teams and personal, simultaneously)

Making strategy is a process.

The day it becomes a procedure you're on your way down. Quite often, I see organisations where making strategy was once a process with brilliant tools to help it. And then somehow, somewhere, it gets institutionalised and becomes a deep-sigh inducing procedure, featuring a prescribed slide deck that must be filled with 85 slides per business unit and knocks all the energy out of the participants. Stop it. Making strategy – certainly with flux being the status quo - is an on going process that can be used to rally people. And it should be a continuous process of testing and validation from a rigorous long-term framework anyway, in keeping with earlier remarks about design – it's evolutionary.

Interdependency

Interdependencies have become truly global over the last twenty years. The progressing deregulation and speed and ease with which companies can do business with each other globally is mindboggling (to me, anyway).

The level of wealth in the Western world has never been higher, even if we factor in the current markdown of the financial crisis. The acceleration in the way technology develops changes how companies and individuals interact fundamentally.

The on-going digitisation of the economy permits us to share information with others any place and anytime we want. The economy is no longer based on the exchange of goods, but increasingly on leveraging business opportunities based on knowledge and information that reside with a specific individual or a group of individuals (an organisation, if you will)

These create emerging themes that in my belief will influence or change the way organizations are operating:

- The way people will continuously search for a balance between work and their private lives, simply because their basic financial security does no longer have to be a real issue;
- The way in which people as consumers have learnt to make their wishes and demands a proactive starting point for making buying decisions. Organisations would *say* that the customer is king, the customer is now *aware* that she is queen and has power over her own destiny. This empowered attitude is finding its way in how organisations should interact, internally, with customers and in labour relations;
- The transparency forced by social media will only drive this further, faster.

The latter translates as follows in my view: the higher the level of education/wealth of an individual, the lower the acceptance for a traditional hierarchical relationship with an organization or being boxed in will be, whether as a client, employee or in another capacity.

This creates interesting challenges for organizations on a meta-level.

- They need to build systems and ways of interacting that facilitate and guarantee agility and adaptability;
- Starting point in entering in to relationships with stakeholders needs to be that they build on the core competencies of an organization;
- There needs to be an absolute focus on sustaining these relationships and converting them in partnerships, based on creating win/win situations;
- A core question becomes how organizations can capitalize on the accumulated tacit knowledge they hold.

In order to remain competitive and be sustainable, when I distil strategically important conditions for succeeding at this, organisations need to have the following ingrained in their systems and structures:

- Openness paired to truthfulness
- The power of aggregation
- Embracing change as constant
- Decisiveness
- Sustainable connection to developments in markets and technology

Openness paired to truthfulness

Increasingly, companies are becoming glass houses, with the free flow of information. This means that I think companies can make a choice: to accept and act according to this de facto reality vs. neglecting it and in the process, probably damaging their own and stakeholders' interests because the perception of their acts will be negative, because they radiate an air of secretiveness.

If they take the positive route, i.e. to interact with stakeholders in an open and truthful manner, within the boundaries of the viable laws and other regulations, this creates a positive perception among stakeholders, which eventually translates in tangible value.

If organisations make the latter choice, this means they cannot normatively proscribe a direction for the development of the organization. It then becomes the result of true interaction with stakeholders. I continue to stress the importance of truthfulness.

The high degree of basic security that people enjoy as a result of generic wealth causes people to ask themselves the question: "Who am I, why do I do things and what do I really want?" in a freer context and with more intensity. The answers to this question are closely related to values, in my belief. These values are determining with which organizations they decide to connect. Stakeholders will thus have a decreasing tolerance for organizations that just "sweet talk" them and fail to produce any congruent behaviour. Interesting result of this way of shaping interaction is that I think it has implications for an organisation's objectives as well. You cannot strive to create a balance between your stakeholders interests if you just have making as much money as possible as a sole objective. In this approach, making money becomes a logical consequence of doing what you do best and with pleasure, as an organization and in turn, as an individual within this organization.

The power of aggregation

In a world that is as dynamic as the one we live in, it has become impossible to have all the knowledge. Because of that, the objective to have the maximum amount of knowledge in a given or various fields, which created the ultimate competitive advantage in the industrial society, has become obsolete in my view. Knowledge per se is obsolete. The power to aggregate it takes over, because knowledge is available in an unparalleled reserve of repositories that have never been more accessible than today. So the company or organisation that has "all" the knowledge has not made itself a more sustainable candidate or a player with more competitive advantage. A company that invests in helping people build new competencies such as putting complex solutions together, building bridges between people, exploring new ways does, in my belief. I like to think that a core strategic capability for organisations is to able to find and combine knowledge and information that create the appealing solutions that clients want, delivered with the highest possible speed.

Embracing change as constant

Flux is the new fixed – if it ever wasn't.

One of the lessons I have learnt from various client and work situations is that it can prove to be a core quality to be able to embrace continuous change as an inspiring constant. The ability to do this, in individuals and the sum of those, an organisation, can be the determining factor for survival. I feel there are two factors that contribute to creating an atmosphere where this is possible. One is communication through open interaction, rather than a top down flow of "information". The other is creating an environment where people have the space to be who they really are or offer them help in discovering this. Starting from your true strengths and being aware of your weaknesses enables you to digest the experience you gain and put it to good use in life and work. Stability is not in your job title, you can find it in yourself. Once you make this discovery, life becomes a lot more effortless. And as a result of that, it becomes possible to see change as something that is inspiring, rather than threatening. You spend 8 hours a day in a work environment. What a waste if you have to leave half of yourself or more at home.

Decisiveness

I feel that organizations should put the responsibility for anything as "low" as possible within organizations, because it creates decisiveness and thus, agility. If people are given responsibility they find awareness of the consequences of their behaviour in assuming it. This creates an environment for (individual) learning and makes it challenging and fun to work somewhere. "Management" adopts a coaching, rather than a normative role. To avoid an environment that spends an inordinate amount of time on touching base, it helps if each individual has responsibilities and objectives that are directly derivative of organizational goals, translated to an individual perspective. If this is the case, nobody can really object to being asked to answer for themselves truthfully in terms of behaviour, results and attitude.

Sustainable connection to developments in markets and technology

A lot of organizations are becoming more and more technology driven. This can prove to be a strength or a weakness. The risk of it becoming a weakness is especially large if in an attempt to follow technology there is no clear connection to market driven organisational objectives. This is why I mention sustainable specifically, because the wealth of technological opportunities can sometimes lead to an uncontrollable surge in directions of knowledge development and a sheer unending amount of propositions towards the market, eventually leading to threatening the continuity of an organization. It is therefore important in my belief to create a clear strategic framework and a clear market driven process to manage this, from inception to periodical evaluation, with budgetary constraints. Two drivers; the development of people in strategy determined knowledge or competence areas and strategy-determined (vertical) market opportunities.

Two really large chunks – volatility & compression

Any organization faces its own specific, complex challenges, but in a for profit organisation, there are two main areas in which they manifest themselves and that always make a contribution to solving these.

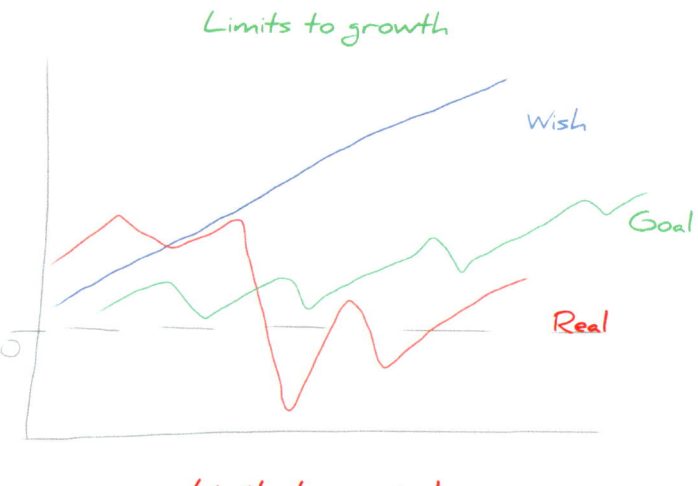

Organizational volatility

The first is linked to a concept I have dubbed organisational volatility. In an organization that is not set up well to deal consistently with its challenges, there is higher volatility in the results and outcomes it begets. As the fictitious graph above serves to show, the happy-clappy scenario ("wish") always projects hockey stick growth, seldom attained.

The realistic scenario ("real") is what often happens in an unfocused and inconsistently managed organization: the growth follows a sketchy pattern, with high peaks and proportionally deep and equally unwelcome valleys or even troughs. A different way of saying it is that what happens under the guise of implementing strategy is actually inconsistent management and being caught by surprise by "the market" or other <fill in blank> excuses. That is rarely the true cause, since organizations that have a solid strategy and are consistently managed to achieve its fulfilment succeed to stretch their upside potential and put a floor in for the downside when they hit rough waters. ("goal").

In other words, you should set your limits to growth (with manageable stretch) and can avoid your limits to survival.

Compressing processes and execution

The second area where a lot can be won is an outcome of what I described earlier as stacking. In the good early old days of automation and quality management, we learnt to follow the paper trail with discipline. If a problem arose, we'd track it by taking the piece of paper that came up as a signal for a problem through the organisation until we found the root of the problem. Not to blame-storm, but to improve. It is astounding what you can find when you apply this. It is also a brilliant way to avoid "flavour *du jour*" solutions in automating processes, thus often contributing to perpetuating a SISO[xviii] operation: there's a problem, a software vendor happens to stop by with the latest greatest suite in XYZ process management software, we buy it, implement it and expect things will get better.

When I ask: "why are you doing X this way?" I often get answers that make me cringe. They are frequently somewhere between "because corporate made us" and "it's the best suite in the industry". So what? If it does not work for you, what stops you from taking a stand?

- What is the problem?
- Is this REALLY the problem we need to solve?
- What are the constraints?

- What is the opportunity cost of leaving this unresolved?
- How is the current process structured?
- Where or why is it flawed?
- How can we improve this?
- Who will be impacted by that?
- How does the optimised process look?
- What contracting do we need to do with other departments and potentially, external partners?
- How can we test and validate this quickly?

This is not rocket science and the core can be analysed in under two hours ON PAPER OR A WHITEBOARD if a good representation of all stakeholders is present.

Only after you have executed this step, you can start thinking about automating it. Otherwise you end up with four concurrent CRM systems that aren't talking to each other, require quadruple data entries and a Ph.D. in database architecture to extract and use data on a day-to-day basis. This is not a joke, but sadly a live example from a client organisation.

Applied Common Sense. Most of us are born with it, or learn it from a (grand)parent, but somehow often also learn to check it at the door when walk into our office buildings. Bring it back please. Reward it generously when you see it. It will help you compress processes and execution in time and reduce complexity greatly.

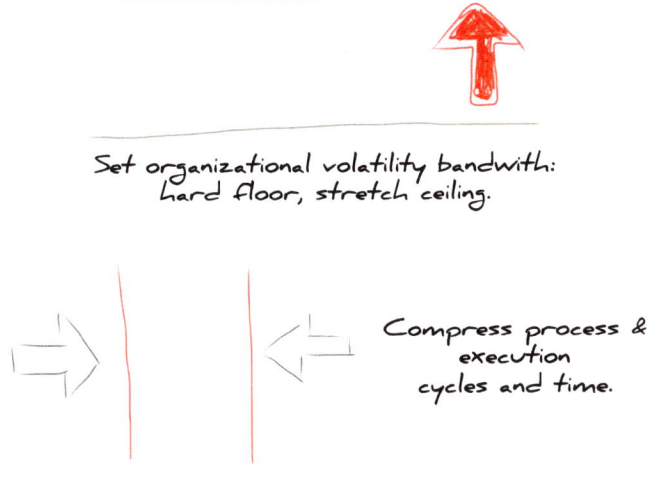

In summary, aligned organizations should be able to set and impose organizational volatility bandwidth based on their strategy and continuously monitor their processes through the lens of strategy to see whether these serve their purpose. The fact that Steve Jobs and his team at Apple could and often would start, kill or radically alter a project after a half hour meeting is not acting on a whim for the majority of the cases, it's because they had a deeply ingrained sense of what their strategy is and where they were heading, up to and including getting these two things right with great consistency.[xix]

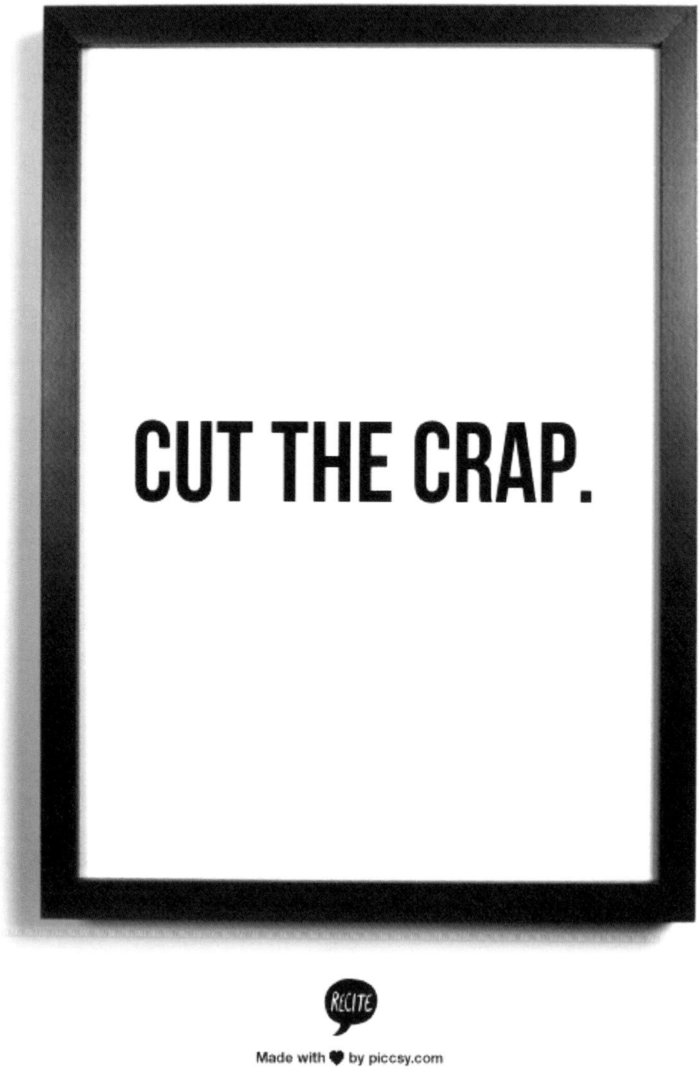
CUT THE CRAP.
RECITE
Made with ♥ by piccsy.com

Face the brutal facts

"That is a very sensitive subject."

"That will not go down well with John/Harriet/Bill (all SVP and up)"

"If that comes to the table, heads will roll."

There's a Dutch saying that goes something like "the soup is rarely eaten as hot as it is served", meaning that even if an issue ruffles people's feathers or makes them feel incredibly ill at ease, often there is just relief once it is discussed openly.

There are always elephants in the room. Naming them and addressing the negative effects they have is one of the absolute core drivers for success in creating change.

The usual pattern is that somebody gets on a soap box, announces the New, New Thing and the expectation is that people adopt it and get on with it.

Often, no credit is given for hard work that has been done, no attention is paid to that deeply painful reorganisation that took place two years ago in which people lost colleagues they valued, let alone that any deep analysis has been made collectively why some structural flaws we agreed we would fix still persist. Not addressing them also drives and compounds stacking.

If you manage to create an environment where the darker stuff can be addressed, you'll find that people are infinitely willing to move forward with almost boundless energy and you will be amazed at what solutions they come forward themselves, often from the most unexpected corners and layers in an organisation.

In our heart of hearts, we all know what we are not bringing to the table. Time to own up to it. Cut the crap = cracking the code. It's not a coincidence that they share the same starting letters, but that would maybe have been too "in your face" as a title. But now you know anyway. ☺

Enough is enough

This is a Bailey bridge. It was probably put up some 65 years ago to temporarily help a bunch of soldiers cross a stream. It still does just that today, even if it isn't necessary anymore. What happens in large corporations is the opposite. We bump into a stream we need to cross. Instead of asking: "where can we get a dingy?" the tendency is to specify a boat in a blueprint. It quickly becomes a coaster and somewhere in the construction process, morphs into a super tanker. This is subsequently placed midstream, as a result of which, we still have not crossed the stream 12 months later and we need to navigate around this massive object to figure out a way to cross that stream after all. Next time: "What's our equivalent of a Bailey bridge for this problem?"

Sit on your hands and bite your tongue.

"Tell me and I will forget. Show me and I will remember. Involve me and I will understand." – Chinese proverb

If you are a senior executive: you may be the smartest guy or gal in the room. You may already have gone through a process that has helped you understand exactly what needs to happen. Time and time again, I have to gently coa(x)(ch) people to not fall into this trap.

You may have a head start, but you turn in it into a loss of ground pretty quickly if you do not give people the opportunity to go through their own process to get their head, hearts and will around something.

And you will be amazed over and over again at what remarkable people and solutions pop up if you let them.

> ### System - How do I stack up?
>
> - What keeps you awake at night?
> - What is the biggest challenge you are facing?
> - What's below the water line?
> - Which elephants are you not naming?
> - What's the real cost of not addressing these issues?

Teams

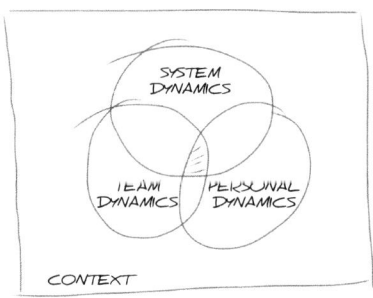

We go to school, where we learn arithmetic, writing and lots of other good stuff. We rarely learn how stuff works between people, let alone how to cooperate. If we're lucky, this happens in a project at university as a by-product.

However, one of the key levers to success for any organisation is the extent to which teams are able to communicate effectively and understand their own dynamics. Being able to (self)assess this is important in completing the picture of context, system dynamics, team dynamics & personal dynamics (as per the model on page 43)

Dr. David Kantor[xx] is originally a psychotherapist who as early as in the late 1950s pioneered a systemic approach to psychotherapy. In addition to that, on a federal grant, he recorded every single interaction in 30 American families during the course of six weeks. He subsequently coded these interactions with a bunch of Ph.D. students and this has yielded us a common language that provides a way to describe human behaviour and characteristics on four levels.

What makes it unique is that it is *observable* so you can name it when you see it in others, as can others when they see you do something. At some time, he came to the realisation that teams in organisations quite often resemble dysfunctional families, so he decided to spend the rest of his career also working in this domain. This is where we clicked.

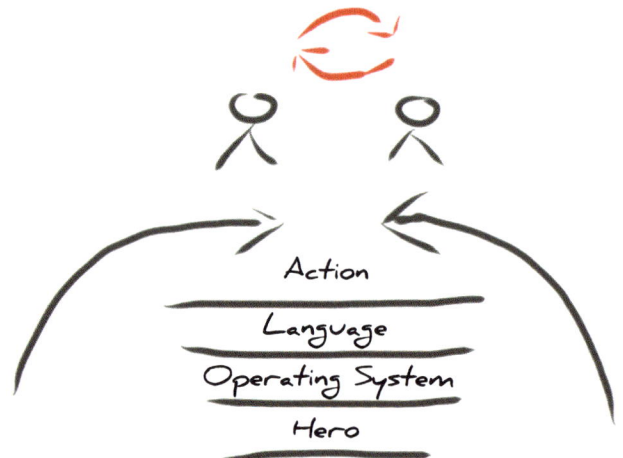

There are 4 levels that play a role when people communicate. The higher the stakes in a given situation, the more layers of your personality come into play.

The psychiatrist Henry Stack Sullivan came up with a brilliant notion to help you think about this. There's GOOD-ME, BAD-ME and NOT-ME.

Good-me is who we would like to be and how we prefer to present ourselves to the world. Bad-me is often closer to who we really are and includes our more shadowy sides and is very often, how others see us. Not-me is the part of us that we usually tend to shield off because it relates to parts of our unconscious that are too whatever to touch upon frequently, let alone share them with the rest of the world.

If you look at this from a slightly more Jungian perspective, you could say that everyone has a light and a shadow side to their personalities. Dependant on the situation, people will react to what happens lightly or more from their shadowy side. A highly determining influence is the extent to which someone feels that the situation is "high stakes" for him or her. Having a cup of coffee with your mom in the mall (if you don't have big issues left between you): pretty low stakes. Having an argument with your life partner: pretty high stakes. A dysfunctional relationship with your boss: high stakes too. The higher the stakes, the more levels come into play. On both sides, or in all people, if you are in a group.

Before all other levels, we are where your personal story starts, your core, if you will. It can be captured in two stories: a Story of Perfect Love and a Story of Imperfect Love, in roughly seven billion highly personal varieties. They will have started when you were a child, where in the first five to seven years of your life you will hopefully have experienced bliss, almost as though the world just existed and unfolded for you. You will inevitably also have been bitterly disappointed a first time, or several times. This is your Story of Imperfect Love.

Level 1 is the Action domain. People Move, Follow, Oppose and Bystand. One of the most interesting levels is Level 2, Language. You thought you spoke English. You do. But you also speak in Power, Affect or Meaning. This is one of the core reasons why people often exclaim things like: "Am I not speaking English or something?!? You are just soooo not getting it!" Level 3 is your Operating System. You either do things in an Open, Closed or a Random way. Level 4: out of your core, you develop a sort of heroic mode. You become a Fixer, a Survivor or a Protector.

Because as in any game, the higher you get, the harder it becomes, we'll start to work with Level 1.

Level 1 – Action domain

A different way to look at relationships, between lovers, a family or a team, is to view them as living systems. When you do that, it allows you to take distance and hover over them, almost as if you were in a helicopter.

In such living systems, people take positions all the time when they interact.

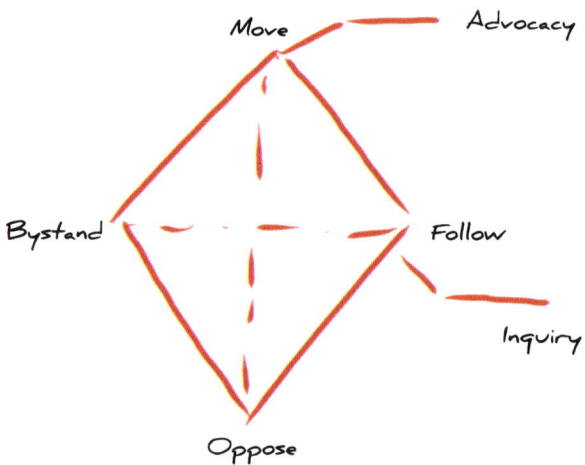

RECAP: in a healthy system, each of these four positions is present in a more or less balanced way. Why? Without **movers**, there's no action. Without **followers**, there's no completion. Without **opposers**, there's no correction. And without **bystanders**, there's no perspective.

Each of these perspectives can present themselves in a healthy or a less healthy way.

A couple of examples to get an impression:

MOVE

"Our team event is coming up. Let's go for a bike ride together."

FOLLOW

Sure. I'll rent the bikes.

OPPOSE

"I'm not sure that's a good idea. Looks like it will rain on Thursday."

BYSTAND

"I see you want to go for a bike ride, John's willing to organise it and Bill says he doesn't wanna do it because it might rain. What could we do to mitigate that risk?"

Each person has typically got a STRONG, a weak and a **STUCK** position. As an example: you can be a strong mover. That makes it likely that you can be a weak follower (you like taking the initiative after all) and it could also mean that you are a stuck opposer (you dig in, because "they" are not following your initiative).

Level 2 - Language

You thought you spoke English. And you do. But you also speak in:

- Power
- Affect
- Meaning

This is one of the core reasons why people often exclaim things like: "Do you not speak English or something?!? You are just soooo not getting it!"

To get your head around this: which of the following questions speaks to you the strongest? Imagine that you are confronted with a high stakes situation.

a) What can we do? (gut: power)
b) How does this feel? (heart: affect)
c) What does this mean? (head: meaning)

A few examples...

Your boss is oriented towards power. You are more oriented towards meaning. You are working on a project and in the middle of writing a report about it. Your boss walks in and says:

"You done with that report yet?"

"Nope, not really. I have done some market research. The data look promising for the new product. But I need some more time to analyze them and write my conclusions."

"That's not what I was asking. When is it done?"

"Well… eur… I guess I could deliver on it in about two days."

"Geez…sometimes you are just way too academic!"

And walks out the door, leaving you feeling bad.

You are in a committed relationship. You are oriented towards affect. Your partner is meaning oriented. You start a conversation.

"This is hard for me. I feel really sad and confused. Lately, I have been feeling that you take me for granted."

"I don't understand what you mean?"

"I've been feeling really neglected. You are never there, and when you are there, you never share anything you feel with me."

"That is objectively NOT true! We had this discussion two months ago. After that, I cut back on my evening engagements by 50%. And I made a serious effort to tell you more about what I am working on and thinking about!"

"You are so insensitive!"

And you flick the light switch and turn your back on your partner.

Level 3 - Operating Systems

To continue the metaphor of computers: just like they have operating systems, so do we. And like there are Linux, Windows and Mac OS, we usually operate on three types:

OPEN
RANDOM
CLOSED

Everybody who's ever used computers in a professional setting intuitively understands that as a general rule, unless somebody makes an effort and writes special code, computers working on one operating system have difficulties -sometimes it's even impossible- communicating with each other. Yet most people are not aware that they frequently clash with other people because, well… they just have different operating systems.

People with a **RANDOM** orientation: you value individual freedom. You're are (described as) creative. You don't do anything in a particular order. You like to move forward fast. Sometimes you find it hard to deal with authority and hierarchy. You like trying or even creating new things. On the flip side, when you come under pressure, people may perceive you as totally unstructured, veering towards anarchic.

People with a **CLOSED** orientation: you like things to be neat and organized. People appreciate you for being orderly, structured and professional. You like delivering on target. Sometimes you have difficulties relating to people because you don't understand why they just cannot do tasks the way you like to do them. On the flip side, people may perceive you as overly hierarchic and inflexible.

People with an **OPEN** orientation: you foster relationships. You sort of keep the bunch together. You do not like conflicts or confrontation. People value you for your attentiveness and ability to adapt, which smoothens edges and gets things done. On the flip side, sometimes you get stuck in processes too much: you succumb to the tyrannical side of democracy and analysis.

Level 4 – Heroic Mode

As we have seen earlier, from early childhood on, we form our own personal stories that help us define our perspective on the world and ourselves, sometimes even our very sanity. In these personal myths and life's journey, the archetypes that we hold on to, or let ourselves be defined by in high stakes situations, play a substantial role. Since your life is a story, you are quite allowed to see yourself as the hero in it. That's why these archetypes are also called your "Heroic Mode". There are three:

- The Fixer
- The Survivor
- The Protector.

Each has a light, a grey and a dark zone. In the light zone this mode is what makes you feel alive, authentic and real. In the dark zone, mostly brought out in high stakes situations, this is what connects you to your own dark side that you have built up since childhood, your demons, if you will.

	Fixer	Survivor	Protector
Light	Fixes	Endures	Shields
Dark	Boundaries	Abandons	Blame

The Fixer has a deep drive to preserve harmony, so s/he fixes things. On the dark side, we could add the by-line: … at any cost. This is why when the fixer gets into hot water, s/he has a tendency to cross boundaries. ("Wall? Which wall? I do not see a wall?" and then bulldozers through it.) The Survivor usually has a long-term goal in mind and focus, so does not mind navigating and making some concessions along the way. Until… it's enough. On the grey end, Survivors are good at checking out mentally. On the dark side, they abandon. (Seven years of a dysfunctional marriage ends with a sticky note on the fridge: "I am outta here.") Protectors shield who and what is important to them. When that comes under threat, in the dark zone, they will blame others or themselves for failing at that.

It is easy to simplify these things. Each person has some aspects of these three Heroic Modes in her/himself. Only through serious work (e.g. psychotherapy) you will learn the true intricacies of this about yourself. Also, people in business have a strong drive to suppress a lot of this, because they are required (by themselves and each other) to appear temperate and in control….

In order for the light to shine so brightly, the darkness must be present.
SIR FRANCIS BACON

Levels 4 to 1 play a major role in how you behave. Your core is about how you came to be who you are and provides an explanation for and insight in why you have become what you are at all these levels today.

> **Teams - How do I stack up?**
>
> - What was your best team experience?
> - Your worst?
> - How does your current team stack up?
> - Which dynamics do you see (MOVE, FOLLOW, OPPOSE, BYSTAND)?
> - Which dynamics are missing?

Craft #3 – Understanding Team Dynamics

Instead of Bullshit Bingo, play Interaction Bingo.

- Draw out the Move, Follow, Oppose, Bystand diagram on a sheet of paper. (page 95)
- During the meeting, try to score what dynamics you see and which are missing.
- What's the balance between advocacy and inquiry?
- What patterns do you see?
- How functional are they?

Make an Action Layer Team Snapshot

We're much more kinaesthetic than we are aware of sometimes. Creating a spatial rendition of something tends to yield very different insights and opens up a much deeper level of awareness.

- Prepare four sheets of paper that say "MOVE" "FOLLOW" "OPPOSE" "BYSTAND"
- Find or create a space of about 4 sq. m./13 sq. ft. Ask your team members to gather around you in a wide circle.
- Prepare lay them out on the floor as per the diagram on page 95, so in a diamond shape.
- As you place "MOVE" on the floor, say: "Without movers there's no initiative" When you place "FOLLOW" to the right, say: "Without followers, there's no completion". When you put "OPPOSE" at the bottom, say: "Without opposers, there's no correction." Finally, put "BYSTAND" on the left and say: "Without bystanders, there's no perspective".
- Explain: "These four stances are stances anyone takes in human communication and interaction. You do, however, have a natural preference. Certainly if you come under pressure. You have one where you are STRONG and one where you are

WEAK then. Now, go stand where you would be if you do what comes to you naturally. Take your STRONG position." Also take your own.
- What you see now when everybody has taken their place is an instant snapshot of your team's dynamics. Ask everybody to say a few words about why they stand where they stand and invite others to listen. Sample question: "What makes you a mover?"
- Once you have done this, ask people to shift to their WEAK position, saying: "When you come under pressure, what do you not do so well?" Notice what happens to the energy of the group. Often, there's a marked difference. Where they stand firm on their STRONG position, they're often more "shifty" on their WEAK position. Name it if you see it. Elicit some comments and observations from the group.
- Once you're done, have a brief dialogue about what you saw together.
- A really great way to do this was invented by a client of mine whom we had trained. He's an investment manager. He simply carved out half an hour in the weekly deal flow meeting and did this exercise. They immediately found that in the two sub-teams they had for evaluating deals, there wasn't enough "oppose" energy, in other words, not enough challenger quality. So they redistributed members, thus improving the quality of their decision-making about deals.

YOUR PARENTS HAVE MORE INFLUENCE ON YOUR BUSINESS RESULTS THAN YOU DO.

Personal

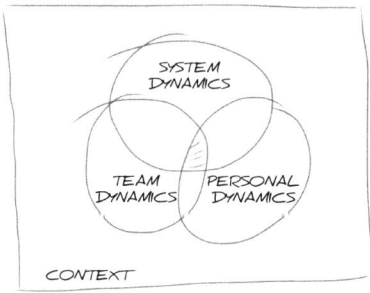

Happy families are all alike; every unhappy family is unhappy in its own way. - Leo Tolstoy

The last element that plays a key role in cracking the code on the four dimensions (context, system, team, personal dynamics) is the extent to which you and your colleagues are aware of and capable to work with each other's personal stories.

Contrary to popular belief, you cannot segment who you are in your work persona and your private persona. If you think you can: think back to a situation where you found yourself drawn in at work. In all honesty, did you respond any differently then when you would if you got drawn in privately?

In assessing leadership, I use the notions of authenticity and congruency, among other things.

I would define authenticity as a key aspect in being able to be an effective leader. If you have done personal work, know who you are, what your purpose is and have strong values, it becomes relatively easy to communicate effectively.

Then there is congruency. I would define this in the simplest terms as walking your talk or "leading effectively also requires modelling the behaviour that you want to engender in others.[xxi]" A leader is both the biggest enabler as well as the biggest blocker for the change she wants accomplish, because whenever she is off the mark on authenticity or congruency, people will use it as an excuse not to adopt the behaviours needed to achieve the goals or not to engage in the necessary activities.

What you also need is good balance, because if you go off the scale on either, you will fail as a leader. Two very crass examples for the sake of clarity: if part of your authenticity is nudism, that's fine, but it will not help the perception of your leadership if you show up in the office stark-bollock naked. Hitler and Goebbels were an extreme example of extreme congruency but with cataclysmic results.

In my own practice I see that whenever senior leadership is not communicating adequately and effectively, it usually finds its roots in lack of congruency and/or authenticity. This tends to have a detrimental effect on organizational performance as a whole.

Your personal story travels with you wherever you go, so it makes sense to do work to find out where it's helping you and where it gets in your way. And to share some of it in your team. It makes you human.

Every time you do that, you forge a closer bond that brings you closer together and closer to cracking the code.

I come from a school of therapy where I learnt that you adopt a first response when you come under pressure that is physically observable. Since you started doing that when you where very young, the chances that you can in some way reprogram yourself to not do that anymore are pretty slim. You can however learn to recognise this when it happens and to take it in and adopt different behaviour. But take it in you must, otherwise you're effectively perpetuating a state of trance that may have worked for you when you were five, but isn't necessarily very useful when you are 35.

To give you an example: based on my background, I respond to stressful situations by being scared. So I freeze and check out. So unless I recognise this, moderate it and thus reset myself, imagine what being in a workshop with me would look like…

I also try to stay close to my core by trying to stay tuned into where I am at, among other things through writing poetry and walking.

Working with your personal story – let alone with that of others- requires a great degree of respect, compassion and the right reflective space. Don't go there if you cannot muster this – for yourself and others.

Health Warning:

You may access domains that profoundly unsettle you if you do this work. If you notice that, please consult a professional about it. It is not a shame if that happens, but rather could prove to be a gift. See a coach, psychologist or therapist if you feel you get that unsettled.

To a Soldier

Atop a bench
In the Park in April
Cigarette and coffee in hand

You said:

" I have seen so much shit.
I have spilt it, seen it ooze from
Friends and foes – from myself-
And let's just forget about the rest.

Who am I to be worthy of love?"

I said:

"There's a man who sits beside me who is.
Worthier than many a man.
You get up every day and start afresh –
With all there was and is.

That may seem a small feat to some.
I know it's not.
Bring yourself – warts and all.
That's enough. That's here, now,
Not yesterday or tomorrow.

You'll know where she is
And what it is.
And yes, it'll sting sometimes.
So what – at least you know
You are alive."

My Day

I buy a bilge pump in the village
Because the pond must be emptied out
Otherwise our children will drown,
Or so my wife has been imploring for a while.

We thought all other
Livestock had been saved
And released.

After the first trial,
I notice two dead and two live
Water salamanders,
Orange, black, freckled, beautiful.

In the end, I save another twelve.

I mess about a little more,
I set them free, in the brook,
Around the corner.

I fetch my children.
Two go to sleep, immediately,
With glowing red cheeks.
The eldest is looking for us.

We listen to him,
At the dinner table. It's late,
But he is here and
He is seen.

I feel guilt about the dead,
Even though there are
Only two of them, today.

It's beautiful:

Death. Guilt. Making up.

And looking for approval.

It's all there. Always.

But I can see it, separate it and: It's okay.

This was my day.

Craft # 4 – Personal (Story) Work

Here, I offer three practices you can use:

- The life line exercise, which you can use individually or share in a group
- Musical Dinner: a gentle way to share a little more about yourself as a team than you normally would.
- Stay tuned – a reflective individual practice you can build to stay more connected to who you are.

Life Line Exercise

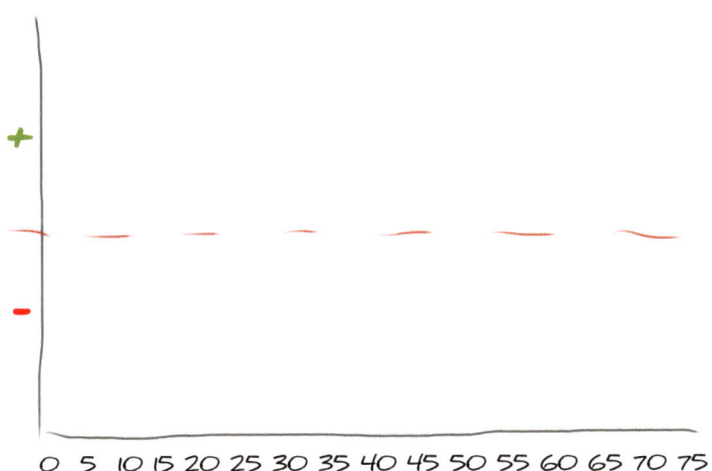

- Copy or draw the diagram.
- Go for a walk in the park, forest, on the beach. Take a notebook.
- Breathe. If your breathing is somewhere around or below your diaphragm, you're ready to find a nice spot to draw and write. If it's somewhere around your chest and up, walk some more and ask yourself what's bugging you. Breathe out.

- Draw the important moments in your life to date. Be gentle on yourself. Mark the highs and lows.
- Connect the dots.
- What patterns do you see?
- What affected you most?
- What do you think is your "first movement" in times of pressure?
- How does this help you?
- Where do you get in your own way?
- Write your story to date. Share it with your life partner or a friend if you want to.
- OPTIONAL: ask your team to join you in this endeavour. Find a good space to share this (your house may be, a room with lots of natural light, a circle of chairs, no tables). Take generous time. Listen to each other. Make it safe.

Musical Dinner

There's hardly a more direct way to people's hearts and spirit than music. I must have hosted or attended well over a hundred of these by now and they are often mesmerising. "If I had known that about you, I never would have..." "That is so remarkable. Now I finally understand..." "This moves me to tears. I was thinking of leaving. Now I'll stay." And sometimes, with all this being present, they also morphed in to some of the longest and coolest party nights I have seen.

Send out an invitation that contains wording similar to this:

"For this dinner please bring a piece of music that is important to you, represents a turning point in your life or symbolizes change for you personally.

Please prepare a story you can tell with this music. Be prepared to share a little more with your colleagues than you normally would while respecting your personal boundaries."

- Pick a restaurant that offers private dining and is OK with you playing your own music there. Instruct the management and the staff to be non-intrusive. They serve only when no music is playing and people are talking amongst themselves, NOT when someone is telling her story.
- Bring a boombox of some sort that let's you connect a PC, mobile, iPod and play music.
- Contract for safety: what happens here, stays here. It's about listening respectfully, not about cracking corny jokes at the expense of others.

- Share your music and your story first. Think about what you want to achieve. The way you bring it sets the tone.
- Let it flow. Whoever wants to go next, goes. Don't pick people.
- Enjoy...

Stay Tuned - Developing a Practice

Find your own way to greet the day. Instead of getting up, running in to the shower, try starting to take five minutes to come into the world again. In other words: tune in. Put your feet firmly on the ground. Breathe. Pace. Try to gauge where you are. Ask yourself how you are doing. Then start the day and worry about your TO DO list. Have you ever tried to make a STOP DOING list, by the way?

Inspiration is in strange places.

When was the last time: you read a book? Poetry? Saw a great concert? Chopped some wood? Painted or drew a picture? Hung out at the Tate? Cooked a great meal and sat down at the table with your loved one(s)? (Microwaving junk from the supermarket doesn't count) Took your shoes off in the park to feel the grass? Wrote some cool stuff yourself?

It's easy to loose it. So stick to it. Somehow. But by all means: find your own way to do it. Some take half an hour in the morning to tune in. Others take half a day a week to walk and talk with a friend to talk about nothing and everything.

Create rituals. Contrary to what religions have often showed us in the past, because they strayed away from their initial pure intentions: people need rituals to come to themselves and turn together. To mark transition. To celebrate. To mourn. To whatever. And eventually, as long as you build them together, you'll find that it becomes irrelevant whether you call this functional, exercise, connecting with the world, yourself, God, Allah, Buddha, Jaweh, the Universe, ... Because it is about creating space for who you really are. And in finding your own way for doing that, you make the world a little more beautiful. Become your own guru.

It brings to mind the story about a man who stopped going to church. Since he was from a strongly Reformed Christian background, soon the minister and elders came by, asking him why he never came to church anymore. He answered them: "I have made a discovery. I do not have to go to church to find God. On Sundays I get up at six and take the dogs for a walk in the forest. It is there that I have a deep sense of belonging to God and the world." They left, puzzled, and left it at that.

Or the story of the Jewish man, whose family was nearly entirely obliterated in the Holocaust, who stopped believing in God. But he continued to observe all the rituals. Because it was his means, as he said, to keep his sanity and to connect with those who were still there, newly born, newly found, and those who had gone.

Or the guy who goes for a run along the beach every day, because it served him well as a substitute for drinking. And it had become to mean much more than that, over the years.

And at the end of a day, take stock. Be gentle on yourself, but take stock. Tune out.

Some ideas for developing a practice

- Keep a journal. Start the day by writing in it. Not for posterity, but for yourself. Write about where you are. Number each day that you write. If you miss a day, starting counting again.
- Promise yourself to find at least two hours a week that are just *your time*. Do whatever you want. Or nothing.
- Make a drawing
- Take a walk around the block every day. Smell the flowers. Spot a cool building you never noticed before. Spot a bird you've never seen before.
- Go for a drive, just for the pleasure of driving. Discover a neighbouring town.
- Get a bike.
- Cook a really different meal. With love. Savour it.
- Go to the garden centre. Buy some flowers and do some instant gardening.
- Invent one yourself.

Notice that there is a form of motion in all of these things. Your brain needs that. In engaging like this, your conscious and subconscious connect. Allowing your brain to rejig things in ways you'll find amazing and shift your energy balance. Pure alchemy. Delivered to your doorstep (almost) for free.

> Personal - How do I stack up?
>
> - How's your energy level lately?
> - How do you think your personal story influences you?
>   - Positively?
>   - Negatively?
> - What are you missing?
> - How do you get into hot water when you come under pressure?

Making it work

Rule # 6.

A prime minister goes visiting to another one. They take the photo opportunity and smile their smiles. An aide closes the double doors. Right when they're about to start talking shop, the double doors blast open again and a man starts gesticulating and delivering a heated point of view. The prime minister looks over his glasses, smiles and says: "John, aren't you forgetting about rule # 6?" The man's face lights up, he smiles, bows out and says: "Thanks, prime minister, that was just what I needed!" The other prime minister is quite puzzled and asks what rule # 6 is. "Oh, it's quite simple", answers the prime minister:

"Rule # 6 is: stop taking yourself so f*cking seriously, will you?"

They both laugh heartily. "And are there any other rules?" "Yeah. There were. But we forgot about them, because this is the most important one."[xxii]

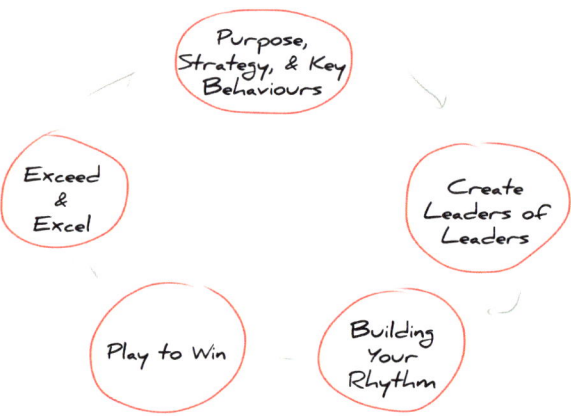

At a high level, whether you do this at the team level or for a whole organisation, the diagram above shows the virtuous cycle or flywheel you are trying to build. Based on the various organisations we've worked together with, I can say that this approach delivers on engaging every employee's leadership from a size range in people from a little over or under a hundred to well over 10,000.

A sample case:

Working with the board and the communications department, we aligned strategy, core purpose and values and developed a coherent storyline to bring it to the company and its stakeholders. With a core team of 3 people we designed a 3-Day Foundational Master Class for 20 selected internal professionals of a 6,000 people company: (informal) leaders from all disciplines. The design of the program was synchronized with business strategy, leadership development programs and restructuring programs alike. Core principle of the program: do it yourself. The program aimed at full DIY realization of a deep cultural change. The 20 internal coaches went through a highly experiential learning program, that also involved designing a physical learning journey. Together with 45 line managers they guided 200 sessions with an average of 10 participants in 10 regions. The throughput time of the process was 4 months. The output of the process was embedded in a tailored action development program that cascaded in a social network savvy way. 6,000 people started changing their company, within the reach of their own field of responsibility and framed within the context of the priorities of the organization.

Results: winning behaviors & capabilities adopted and a common framework to accelerate.

For the sake of simplicity, I will focus here on the questions we typically work with organisations and outline the process. I trust you to be intelligent enough to deduct from this cookbook how this could work at a team level.

Purpose, Strategy & Key Behaviours

Start small

"Something old, something new, something borrowed, something blue…"
English bridal rhyme, early 19th century

The rhyme provides the perfect design criteria for bringing together the small group of people you want to gather to look at this part of the puzzle. Try to stay under 10, probably closer to seven sooner.

- *Something old*: to stand for two to three senior people you trust and have a longstanding connection to the organisation.
- *Something new:* find two to three young guns (who stand out and haven't been around to long to ensure a fresh, non-regimented perspective.
- *Something borrowed:* to mean a trusted (external) facilitator who can guide, hold up a mirror and make sure all the voices are heard.
- *Something blue:* "blue" people in many management style assessments are the people who bring challenging, structure, order and rigour. ("CLOSED" in our language) Since this is no small feat, you want them on board early. **How many women are on your list?** Look harder.

What you want to look at in this session -which can usually be accomplished in about a day and a half- is the following:

- *Slow down* – reflect on what you want the outcome to be individually and your personal, individual values.
- *Make a real connection* – Share your personal stories with each other and explain how they defined your personal values.
- *Company purpose and values* – What is our purpose (why do we exist, not solely for generating profit, to give you an obvious clue) and which values will help us achieve it?

- *Strategy* – What is our strategy and how does it align with our purpose and values?
- *Roadblocks* – What is standing in our way and more importantly, how do we get in our own way?

At some point, next to (re)capturing or even reframing your purpose, values and strategy, you will begin to see what needs to unfold.

One Thing

OK. OK… Maybe two or three. But not more. You are looking for the smallest things that will make the biggest impact. As I indicated in the chapter at the beginning of the book on stacking, people cannot keep focus on much more than one thing outside of their already pressurised and swamped day-to-day environment. In my action research in the last seven years, I have seen that whenever an organisation or a team stretched itself beyond one to three big things next to their day-to-day objectives, they tend to fail at achieving any them. This is now corroborated by the research done for "The Four Disciplines of Execution" by Sean Covey:

Goals next to the Vortex	1-3	4-10	11-20
Goals Achieved	1-3	1-2	ZERO

Bring the whole system in the room.

- How will what we come up with impact the four domains: context, system, teams and individuals?
- How will it reduce fragmentation?
- How will it help us to stop stacking?

Also remember I invited you to take a cybernetic or evolutionary stance towards design.

- What does our prototype look like?
- What's the film we are trying to create?
- How does it begin? What happens? How will it end?
- How can we test and validate our approach?

- What are the two to four key behaviours we need to see to make this happen?

Create Leaders of Leaders

Build a Gang

Whenever we get to this stage, I ask whom the person I am working with wants to have in her gang to make this happen. Depending on the size of an organisation, there are usually 10 to 60 people who always raise their hand anyway when there is something new to do. Senior executives can almost always make a list off the top of their heads. These are the people you want to work with and make a deep investment in. Don't be too polite or discriminate in ruffling a few feathers here and there because some senior people or usual suspects are not on the list.

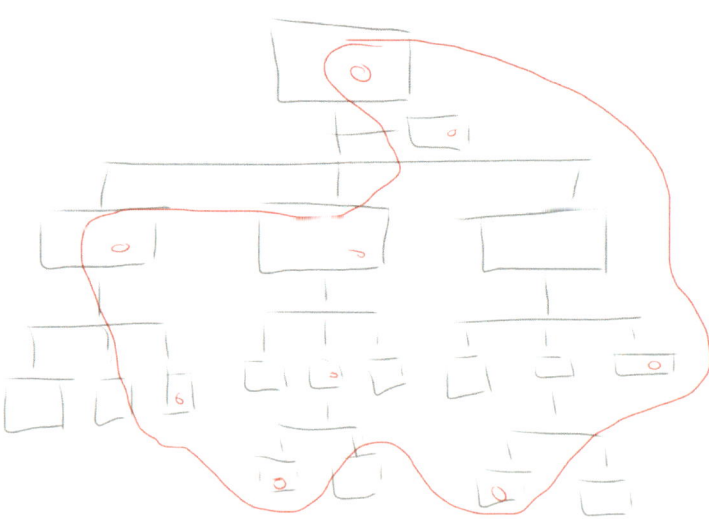

A lens that helps here is the Core Group theory as formulated by Art Kleiner. In essence, he contends that organisations do not necessarily exist to create shareholder value, make the world a better place or whatever their stated drivers are. *They exist first and foremost to serve the interests of a core group of people.* Depending on the integrity of this core group, on the good end of the scale you end up with Whole Foods, Patagonia or Starbucks, on the bad end Worldcom and Enron immediately spring to mind. Have you ever walked into another organisation and noticed that you get a visual body scan from everybody? Do you belong here? Are you in or are you out?

Just taking this on board will help you determine how you can get the maximum reach and street cred for your initiative.

Leverage the power of differences

Somewhere between the work on purpose, strategy and key behaviours and starting to bring together the gang, you have to test what you want to do, because otherwise down the road, you maybe in for unpleasant surprises. I will never forget that we made a film in which we followed a day in the life of a recently retired employee of a company we were working with. He was fully active, helping out to build something, doing sports and enjoying life. He said some very poignant things about leadership in great sports stories and metaphors. Very inspiring.

Or not. It won us the project, but when we were showing the film to accompany explaining what we had co-created with our joint team on the client side, a mechanic who was also on the worker's council upon seeing the film exploded and left the room screaming "This is exactly what we don't have here and these are all the people we have let go in the last years. <several coarse expletives deleted>".

What surfaced when my colleagues talked with him and in later conversations was deep pain about the reorganisations and lay offs that had taken place in the organisation. Once we were able to give this with him, we took it into account in how we would work with that if similar dynamics would surface somewhere else during the process. So once that happened, he joined with such enthusiasm that he became one of the strongest ambassadors for the process and worked as a guide in the programs for all employees. At the end of the cycle he was able to see and come forward with how he had long been pointing his finger at the organisation and how it had made him bitter, but that the process had led him to the insight that he also needed to change his behaviour and stance towards the organisation. Ultimately, he arranged for himself to transfer to a role where he could help young, entering mechanics to survive and thrive in the organisation.

Check your ego at the door. Make space for the dissenters. Listen and learn. Own up to mistakes form the past. Make sure they feel heard and seen. And once they feel that that has happened, they usually join with more passion and energy than you will have seen from many others. Be prepared to adapt things or even throw what you have out of the window. It's supposed to be a *working* hypothesis, after all.

Where are the "difficult" guys?
How many women are on your list?
How many people with a different cultural background are on your list?

You guessed it: look harder!

Once this is done and the final selection is made for the group you want to take this forward, it's time to plan a three to five day deep dive with them. During these days, we train them deeply in the capabilities outlined in this book and work with them to design the journey they want to make.

In doing so, we make sure that it isn't a virus that will be quashed at sometime by the body that needs to adopt it. Some guiding principles:

Work with what is there

"What may seem like an inch for you may feel like a mile for the other." - My mother

When this cascades down, here are some important points:

- People need space to get their heads around what needs to happen, so they need to be able to go through pretty much the same process as the previous groups **BUT** it will be of most value to them and the organisation if it is framed at their own level of influence.
- I hope this book shows that the crafts described in it can be transferred easily, so literally bring these skills down to the "lowest" layer in the organisation. This is where you can deliver on the promise that you can take leadership and its development "down" to every single layer of the organisation.
- Welcome resistance. Friction also generates energy. Find ways to embrace it.
- Make each event a small physical journey. It's hard to imagine movement and change when you are stuck in a chair in a dreary conference room. Normally, our brains operate on beta waves. In a state between waking and sleeping – for example when that big idea hits you in the shower- we're operating on theta 1 waves. When we go outdoors and take a long walk, a train journey or a road trip, our brain starts to work on alpha waves, thus rejigging information in way that connects the right and the left side of our brains.[xxiii] This is where can hit flow. It's also just vastly more inspiring and may turn in to a once in a lifetime experience for people. For the penny pinchers: it's also cheaper. A forest, beach or park do not habitually charge $ 600 per half day for using them as a conference room. What about the weather? Late spring and summer are the ideal times for running this part, since most of the economy slows down anyway. You might as well invest in some major maintenance at that time.

- Use backward planning. Get a great team of "blue" people to craft the logistics of all of this and let them go wild at what they do best: deliver a flawlessly planned and executed process.
- The second world war was in part won by liaison officers. Spot them and let them get on with things. They are invaluable in bringing you qualitative data and a real sense for where things are.
- Truly adopt a DIY approach. Use external facilitators to help you design the process, train you in these crafts and coach and support you, but make your investment in your own people pay. Trust them to deliver it as best as they can. There's no more powerful catalyst for getting people to embrace change than learning new things and getting great insights from a colleague: she's in the same boat.

Build Your Rhythm

"Insanity is doing the same thing over and over again and expecting different results." – Albert Einstein

Verne Harnish always says "A rhythm will set you free" and uses the analogy of jazz musicians: you may be Japanese and I may be Dutch, so we do not speak the same language but we can convey to each other in which key we'll play. Once we know that, we can jam…

Teams – in general, but in this process in particular- should take a good hard look at themselves and assess whether their rhythm fosters getting the output and results they want. 10:1 that in most cases, if you are brutally honest, it's based on conventions, input driven and not as effective as it could be.

In the process, it's important to also look at what rhythm teams operate on. Do they even know they have one? An important outcome of spending a day or two half days together should be:

STOP – START – MORE

How are we getting in our own way as a team? Having seen and understood what is expected of us, what are we going to STOP doing? What are we to START doing? What are we going to do MORE? How are we going to keep SCORE? What's our focus the next 90 days? How will we keep the organisation in the loop?

A few clues: less e-mail, less conference calls, less communication through department head A to B to bitch and moan about the white space between department A and B. Pick up the phone. Reach out. Walk over. Have a coffee. Get lunch. Co-mu-ni-ca-te di-rect-ly.

Play to Win

The Bicycle Repair Shop Award

Some time ago, I worked with the management team of an IT department of an organisation where it was a core business driver and condition sine qua non for the daily operation. They had a range of 120 problems that just would not go away. In an afternoon, we analysed and chunked them in four buckets. We crafted tailor made solution ranges for all of them. In the largest chunk, we found some common constraints that made the problems persist: employees did not feel empowered to resolve them. We removed the organisational roadblocks for this, set clear boundaries for when and how employees could act independently without consulting management: under x $, go ahead, if operational risk = constrained to ..., proceed.

We then instituted the Bicycle Repair Shop Award, after the analogy of pitching up at your local village repair shop with a small problem, the repair man fixing it in a few minutes. You ask: "Do I owe you something for this?" And he answers: "Nah, no worries. You're a good customer." Precisely the behaviour we wanted to inspire.

The prize: a simple dinner with your core team or your family. People could submit candidates and kept score together.

Net result after 90 days: 7 problems yet to resolve, rest gone. New behaviours adopted & embedded, client satisfaction up 30%.

Core elements to Play to Win:

- Analyse the problem at a systemic level making good use of the work already done, get teams to build on what they find in the first cycles;
- Get them to involved to set the behaviours and boundaries and make them very transparent through an appealing story or metaphor;
- "Game" the process;
- Get people to keep score and engage their competitiveness;
- Offer small but meaningful rewards;
- Sit back and enjoy the show.

Exceed & Excel

Look for ways to continuously reinforce and embed by giving people space to run.

You know it when you see it, but quite often, if you create the culture for it, people just come and bring it to you:

"Whole Foods is built on the idea that we want to encourage the creativity and intelligence of every one of our team members. If I could draw back the curtain, what you would see is a very strong culture of empowerment, and that is the secret of Whole Foods. We have these 78,000 fantastic team members who have a little room to run, and that is the strength of the company, the culture, which is the living, breathing heart of the company."

"Everybody in Whole Foods, including John and me, belong to a team. That's the first thing, the basic human desire to belong and be part of something larger than yourself. In Whole Foods, labour is a fixed cost, not a variable cost as it is in other operators. If a team can generate revenue that exceeds a budgeted margin between the revenue and labour cost, they share in the gain. Every 30 days it's in their paycheck. If the build sales or safe costs, the productivity they create is shared with them. We're doing it together. On average in the company last year it was over $1 per hour in their paychecks from gain-sharing, which they created through their own efforts."

"[An example of how this creates innovation is] a customer who had a blind 7-year old son said her son wanted to be able to shop Whole Foods. So a marketing team leader in Thousnd Oaks, CA, created Braille tags so this customer's son could shop. Now those tags have been picked up by the Braille Institute in Boston and are being spread around. She did it on her own – didn't ask permission, just did it. That's the type of thing that builds the company culture."

"Peter Drucker said famously years ago that culture eats strategy for [breakfast]. If you can empower people so they are creating innovations on a constant basis, the company's moving much faster. In the 21st century, distributed intelligence and distributed decision-making is the way to proceed because you're going to go faster. Anything we do in retail can be copied right away – take a picture, send it, boom! The enduring competitive advantage I steam members imbued with a sense of mission who are carrying the company forward. That is a sustainable competitive advantage."
Walter Robb, co-CEO Whole Foods.[xxiv]

Allow yourself 15 months for this complete cycle: three months to prepare, a year to run it, ideally coinciding with your natural planning cycle.

Rinse. Repeat. Lean in[xxv] and stay tuned. Thank you for reading me out.

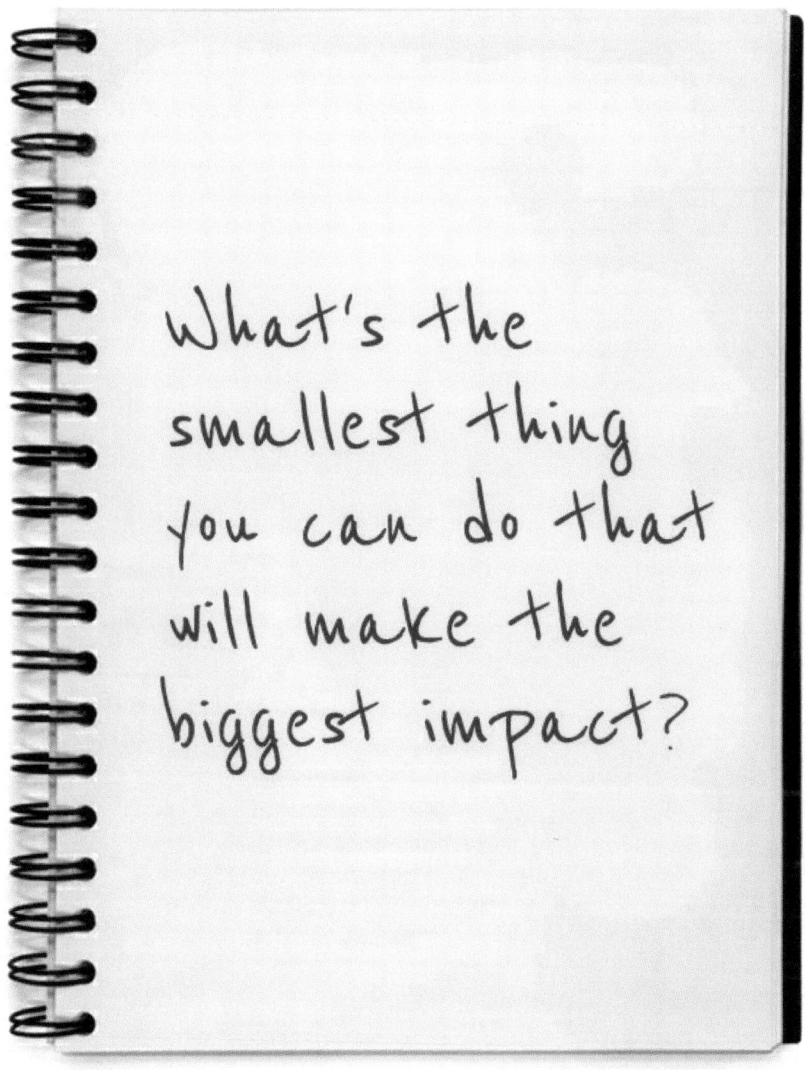

About the author

Martijn has been fascinated by how relationships and dynamics work between people since his youth. David Ogilvy –one of the original "Mad Men"- has strongly influenced his deep interest for future visioning and commercial entrepreneurship and was Martijn's first mentor.

After working as a supply chain manager, business unit manager of large IT consulting firms and ending up in Post-M & A integration, he focuses his professional practice on human dynamics and change.

As a facilitator he works intensively with the life changing work of David Kantor, a master family therapist from the US, and Martijn's mentor for many years. Martijn has developed a specialist practice in transforming human dynamics in the real business context of organizations. He is a gifted process and program designer for large-scale change initiatives and leadership journeys. He facilitates change with role-modeling that suits the context & needs of clients.
He has a longstanding connection to national politics and is regularly consulted on renewal and change by some of the most senior people in Dutch government.

While working with large corporate clients Martijn further developed his way of working, a school of change consulting strongly linked to Peter Senge's original MIT Center for Organizational Learning.

He is the editor of the Dutch edition of "Presence" by Peter Senge, Joe Jaworski, Otto Scharmer & Betty Sue Flowers and "Who Really Matters: The Core Group" by Art Kleiner. Martijn speaks six languages and works in Dutch, English, German and French.

Martijn took a BBA in Rotterdam and has obtained a wide array of post-grad training, among other things in strategic dialogue and systemic therapy. He is married and father to 3 children. He is interested in photography, cooking, travelling and is a voracious reader. He actively supports various charitable causes.

He currently works for Mannaz as one of its client directors.

Mannaz is a frontrunner in leadership development. We design and deliver executive and project leadership programmes for clients across the world. Using our innovative and efficient learning methods, we empower people and organisations to improve performance and business results.

www.mannaz.com

Recommended further reading

On Dialogue

On Dialogue, David Bohm et al.
Dialogue & The Art of Thinking Together, Bill Isaacs

On Systems Thinking & Scenarios

The Fifth Discipline, Peter Senge
The Fifth Discipline Fieldbook, Peter Senge et al.
The Answer To How is Yes, Peter Block

A Whole New Mind, Dan Pink

The Three Tensions, Dodd & Favaro
Scenario Planning in Organisations, Thomas Chermack

On Strategy

Good Strategy, Bad Strategy, Richard Rumelt
Strategy Safari, Mintzberg

On Teams

My Lover, Myself, Dr. David Kantor
Leaders on the Couch, Manfred Kets de Vries
Five Dysfunctions of a Team, Lencioni
Who Really Matters: The Core Group, Art Kleiner
Drive, Dan Pink

On Personal Work

The Seven Habits of Highly Effective People, Stephen Covey
The Work, Byron Katie
Hold Me Tight, Dr. Sue Johnson

Consulted literature:

Business Dynamics, Systems thinking and modelling for a complex world, Sterman, 2001, Irwin/McGraw-Hill

Psychology, Bernstein et al., Houghton-Mifflin, 1999

Serious Play, Michael Schrage, HBS Press, 2000

Dialogue and the Art of Thinking Together, Bill Isaacs, Currency/Doubleday, 1999

Psychosynthesis, Assagioli, Pyschosynthesis Research Foundation, 1965

Grammars of Creation, George Steiner, Faber & Faber, 2001

Who Really Matters: the Core Group, Art Kleiner, Doubleday, 2003

Creativity, Mihaly Csikszentmihaly, Harper Perennial, 1997

The Fifth Discipline, Peter Senge, Crown Publishers, 1990

Fifth Discipline Fieldbook, Peter Senge et al., N. Brealey Publishers, 1998

The Dance of Change, Peter Senge et al., N. Brealey Publishers, 2000

The Irrational Executive, Psychoanalytical Studies in Management, M. Kets de Vries, Edit., Intl. University Press, 1986

Struggling with the Demon, Essays on Individual and Organisational Irrationality, Psychosocial Press, 2000

The Leader on the Couch, M. Kets de Vries, Jossey-Bass, 2006

Maslov on Management, A. Maslov et al. (posth.), Wiley, 1998

Delivering Happiness, Tony Hsieh, galley copy, 2010

Maverick, Ricardo Semler, Warner, 1993
The Seven Day Weekend, Ricardo Semler, Penguin, 2003

My Lover, Myself, Self-Discovery Through Relationship, David Kantor, 2000Inside The Family, David Kantor & William Lehr, 1975

Intimate Environments: Sex, Intimacy and Gender in Families, David Kantor & Barbara Okun, 1989
The Circle of Innovation, Tom Peters, First Vintage Editions, 1999

Creative Destruction, R. Foster & S. Kaplan, Currency/Doubleday, 2001

Vital Lies, Simple Truths, The Psychology of Self-Deception, Daniel Goleman, Bloomsbury 1997

Presencing, Peter Senge, Joe Jaworski, Otto Scharmer, Betty Sue Flowers, Doubleday, 2004

Theory U, C. Otto Scharmer, Berrett-Koehler, 2009

Flawless Consulting, Peter Block, 1987
The Anwer To How is Yes, Peter Block, Berrett-Koehler, 2002

Articles:

Dialogue – A Proposal, David Bohm, Donald Factor, Peter Garrett, 1991

Appreciative Inquiry in Organisational Life, D. Cooperrider & S. Srivastva, 1987

Advances in Appreciative Inquiry as an Organisational Development Intervention, Gervase R. Bushe, Organisational Development Journal, 1995
5 Theories of Change Embedded in Appreciative Inquiry, Gervase R. Bushe, 1998

How we went digital without a strategy, Ricardo Semler, HBR, 09/10-2000

Photography/image credits:

Poster Quotes, unless otherwise stated: © Martijn Sjoorda, images produced through **www.recitethis.com**

Page 7: KLPD
Page 8: Ogilvy Worldwide
Page 13: Arthur Sasse/UPI
Page 16: Boise
Page 49: Aerophoto Schiphol
Page 61: Simon Douglas

All other images made by the author. Models copyright of their respective authors, as cited in the text or under Notes.

Notes

[i] Interview/profile in the New Yorker Magazine, August 2012
[ii] The Four Disciplines of Execution, FranklinCovey
[iii] "Motivating People – Getting Beyond Money", Nov 2009 McKinsey Quarterly
[iv] IBM CEO Surveys, various HBR articles on innovation
[v] "The Fifth Discipline", Peter Senge, Crown Publishing, 1990, and subsequent works
[vi] David Kolb's Experiential Learning: Experience as the source of learning and development (1984)
[vii] Some of the preceding text and concepts were drawn from an unpublished manuscript by me called "Martijn's Model" from 2002-2004
[viii] Some of the preceding text and concepts were drawn from an unpublished manuscript by me called "Martijn's Model" from 2002-2004
[ix] Total number of people involved in programs co-designed with why* consulting customers or one of its preceding affiliates.
[x] The theory of constraints (TOC) is an overall management philosophy introduced by Eliyahu M. Goldratt in his 1984 book titled *The Goal*, that is geared to help organizations continually achieve their goals.[1] Goldratt adopted the concept with his book *Critical Chain*, published 1997. The concept was extended to TOC with respectively titled publication in 1999. An earlier propagator of the concept was Wolfgang Mewes[2] in Germany with publications on *power-oriented management theory* (Machtorientierte Führungstheorie, 1963) and following with his *Energo-Kybernetic System (EKS, 1971)*, later renamed *Engpasskonzentrierte Strategie*[3] as a more advanced *theory of bottlenecks*. The publications of Wolfgang Mewes are marketed through the FAZ Verlag, publishing house of the German newspaper *Frankfurter Allgemeine Zeitung*. However, the paradigm *Theory of constraints* was first used by Goldratt. (Source: Wikipedia) See also Bruce Lewin's Theory of Change as formulated in the 1940s in various publications, in which he addresses constraints explicitly as a lens in making a force field analysis.
[xi] Dialogue – A Proposal, David Bohm, Donald Factor, Peter Garrett, 1991, model adapted from C. Otto Scharmer, 1995, idem Dialogue and the Art of Thinking Together, Bill Isaacs, Currency/Doubleday, 1999
[xii] Chris Parker et al., MTI
[xiii] Management of the Absurd, Richard Farson, 1997, Touchstone Books
[xiv] The Cybernetic Brain, Andrew Pickering, 2010, University of Chicago
[xv] dictionary.com
[xvi] Adapted from a model as introduced by Bill Isaacs and Peter Senge
[xvii] After Richard Rumelt in "Good Strategy, Bad Strategy", 2011, Crown Business

[xviii] Shit IN, Shit OUT

[xix] Walter Isaacson, Steve Jobs biography, 2012

[xx] While I wrote this book and the text is mine, the methodology described in the "Teams" chapter is based largely on the work of Dr. David Kantor, Ph.D. He is the founder and director of the Kantor Family Institute; a postgraduate training institute in the Boston area. He has taught at Harvard, Harvard University Medical School and Tufts University Medical School. He consults to industry, clinical faculties and university-based groups. He started out work as a therapist. During the course of his career, which spans more than fifty years -and he has no intention of ending it any time soon- he also became interested in how organizations work and often, do not work. He has built an enormous body of work around this and is a very important influence for me here and in understanding relationship structures and how one's personal structure enters into important relationships. To his great credit, he has created a whole language, which I rely on heavily in this book. This common language can easily be learnt to better understand yourself and others, build common ground, or more importantly, rediscover it together when you have lost it. This, as this book hopes to show, often generates high impact breakthroughs in important relationships.

[xxi] JC Hewitt in an answer on Quora about leadership

[xxii] A story from a book created for a Unilever Leadership & Growth Conference that I helped organise and facilitate.

[xxiii] This is a vastly simplified rendition of how our brain works and technically not entirely correct: creativity does not solely reside on the right side of your brain nor do your analytical skills find themselves in the left side of your brain, but there is recent research (Neuroscience Faculty, University of Chicago, 2010) that shows that this is how this works. Apart form that, my own action research on and experience with impact shows consistently that when we involve a journey component in a program, the lasting impact and willingness to change behaviour is much larger than when we do it on site or in a conference room.

[xxiv] Fortune Volume 167, number 7, May 20th issue

[xxv] **www.leanin.org**

CPSIA information can be obtained
at www.ICGtesting.com
Printed in the USA
LVIC06n2247271114
415884LV00002B/13